NEW DIRECTIONS FOR CHILD DEVELOPMENT

Maternal Depression and Infant Disturbance

Edward Z. Tronick, Tiffany Field, *Editors*

Maternal Depression and Infant Disturbance

Edward Z. Tronick, *Editor*
University of Massachusetts

Tiffany Field, *Editor*
University of Miami

NEW DIRECTIONS FOR CHILD DEVELOPMENT
WILLIAM DAMON, *Editor-in-Chief*
Clark University

Number 34, Winter 1986

Paperback sourcebooks in
The Jossey-Bass Social and Behavioral Sciences Series

Jossey-Bass Inc., Publishers
San Francisco • London

Edward Z. Tronick, Tiffany Field (eds.).
Maternal Depression and Infant Disturbance.
New Directions for Child Development, no. 34.
San Francisco: Jossey-Bass, 1986.

New Directions for Child Development
William Damon, *Editor-in-Chief*

Copyright © 1986 by Jossey-Bass Inc., Publishers
and
Jossey-Bass Limited

Copyright under International, Pan American, and Universal Copyright Conventions. All rights reserved. No part of this issue may be reproduced in any form—except for brief quotation (not to exceed 500 words) in a review or professional work—without permission in writing from the publishers.

New Directions for Child Development is published quarterly by Jossey-Bass Inc., Publishers (publication number USPS 494-090). *New Directions* is numbered sequentially—please order extra copies by sequential number. The volume and issue numbers above are included for the convenience of libraries. Second-class postage paid at San Francisco, California, and at additional mailing offices. POSTMASTER: Send address changes to Jossey-Bass Inc., Publishers, 433 California Street, San Francisco, California 94104.

Editorial correspondence should be sent to the Editor-in-Chief, William Damon, Department of Psychology, Clark University, Worcester, Massachusetts 01610.

Library of Congress Catalog Card Number LC 85-644581

International Standard Serial Number ISSN 0195-2269

International Standard Book Number ISBN 1-55542-997-1

Cover art by WILLI BAUM

Manufactured in the United States of America

Ordering Information

The paperback sourcebooks listed below are published quarterly and can be ordered either by subscription or single copy.

Subscriptions cost $40.00 per year for institutions, agencies, and libraries. Individuals can subscribe at the special rate of $30.00 per year *if payment is by personal check*. (Note that the full rate of $40.00 applies if payment is by institutional check, even if the subscription is designated for an individual.) Standing orders are accepted.

Single copies are available at $9.95 when payment accompanies order. (California, New Jersey, New York, and Washington, D.C., residents please include appropriate sales tax.) For billed orders, cost per copy is $9.95 plus postage and handling.

Substantial discounts are offered to organizations and individuals wishing to purchase bulk quantities of Jossey-Bass sourcebooks. Please inquire.

Please note that these prices are for the academic year 1986-1987 and are subject to change without notice. Also, some titles may be out of print and therefore not available for sale.

To ensure correct and prompt delivery, all orders must give either the *name of an individual* or an *official purchase order number*. Please submit your order as follows:

Subscriptions: specify series and year subscription is to begin.
Single Copies: specify sourcebook code (such as, CD1) and first two words of title.

Mail orders for United States and Possessions, Latin America, Canada, Japan, Australia, and New Zealand to:
Jossey-Bass Inc., Publishers
433 California Street
San Francisco, California 94104

Mail orders for all other parts of the world to:
Jossey-Bass Limited
28 Banner Street
London EC1Y 8QE

New Directions for Child Development Series
William Damon, *Editor-in-Chief*

CD1 *Social Cognition,* William Damon
CD2 *Moral Development,* William Damon
CD3 *Early Symbolization,* Howard Gardner, Dennie Wolf

CD4   *Social Interaction and Communication During Infancy,* Ina Č. Užgiris
CD5   *Intellectual Development Beyond Childhood,* Deanna Kuhn
CD6   *Fact, Fiction, and Fantasy in Childhood,* Ellen Winner, Howard Gardner
CD7   *Clinical-Developmental Psychology,* Robert L. Selman, Regina Yando
CD8   *Anthropological Perspectives on Child Development,* Charles M. Super, Sara Harkness
CD9   *Children's Play,* Kenneth H. Rubin
CD10 *Children's Memory,* Marion Perlmutter
CD11 *Developmental Perspectives on Child Maltreatment,* Ross Rizley, Dante Cicchetti
CD12 *Cognitive Development,* Kurt W. Fischer
CD13 *Viewing Children Through Television,* Hope Kelly, Howard Gardner
CD14 *Childrens' Conceptions of Health, Illness, and Bodily Functions,* Roger Bibace, Mary E. Walsh
CD15 *Children's Conceptions of Spatial Relationships,* Robert Cohen
CD16 *Emotional Development,* Dante Cicchetti, Petra Hesse
CD17 *Developmental Approaches to Giftedness and Creativity,* David Henry Feldman
CD18 *Children's Planning Strategies,* David Forbes, Mark T. Greenberg
CD19 *Children and Divorce,* Lawrence A. Kurdek
CD20 *Child Development and International Development: Research-Policy Interfaces,* Daniel A. Wagner
CD21 *Levels and Transitions in Children's Development,* Kurt W. Fischer
CD22 *Adolescent Development in the Family,* Harold D. Grotevant, Catherine R. Cooper
CD23 *Children's Learning in the "Zone of Proximal Development,"* Barbara Rogoff, James V. Wertsch
CD24 *Children in Families Under Stress,* Anna-Beth Doyle, Dolores Gold, Debbie S. Moscowitz
CD25 *Analyzing Children's Play Dialogues,* Frank Kessel, Artin Göncü
CD26 *Childhood Depression,* Dante Cicchetti, Karen Schneider-Rosen
CD27 *The Development of Reading Skills,* Thomas H. Carr
CD28 *Children and Computers,* Elisa L. Klein
CD29 *Peer Conflict and Psychological Growth,* Marvin W. Berkowitz
CD30 *Identity in Adolescence: Processes and Contents,* Alan S. Waterman
CD31 *Temperament and Social Interaction,* Jacqueline V. Lerner, Richard M. Lerner
CD32 *Early Experience and the Development of Competence,* William Fowler
CD33 *Children's Intellectual Rights,* David Moshman

Contents

Editors' Notes 1
Edward Z. Tronick, Tiffany Field

1. The Transmission of Maternal Disturbance to the Infant 5
Edward Z. Tronick, Andrew F. Gianino, Jr.
The Mutual Regulation Model offers an explanation for the way in which infants of depressed mothers may develop affective disorders.

2. Epidemiological Perspectives on Maternal Depression and the Young Child 13
William T. Garrison, Felton J. Earls
A review of the epidemiology of maternal depression and infant disturbance looks at new data that question old truths about their relation.

3. Face-to-Face Interactions of Depressed Mothers and Their Infants 31
Jeffrey F. Cohn, Reinaldo Matias, Edward Z. Tronick, David Connell, Karlen Lyons-Ruth
New studies on the distortions of the interaction between infants and their depressed mothers demonstrate the derailment of infants' patterns of engagement.

4. Models for Reactive and Chronic Depression in Infancy 47
Tiffany Field
Depression in infancy and the process that produces it are illuminated by new detailed observational studies of the interactive process.

5. The Depressed Mother and Her One-Year-Old Infant: Environment, Interaction, Attachment, and Infant Development 61
Karlen Lyons-Ruth, David Zoll, David Connell, Henry U. Grunebaum
New research demonstrates the relation of infant attachment behaviors and cognitive competence to maternal depression.

Index 83

Editors' Notes

Evidence has accumulated that maternal depression is related to affective and cognitive disturbance in infants. This volume presents reviews and recent research on the effects of maternal depression on infants and young children. It includes reviews of the epidemiology of maternal depression, studies on the distortions of interactions between depressed mothers and their infants, models for reactive and chronic depression in infancy, and research demonstrating the effects of maternal depression on infant attachment behavior and cognitive competence.

The first chapter, by Tronick and Gianino, presents the "Mutual Regulation Model," which offers a possible explanation for the way in which infants of depressed mothers may develop affective disorders. The authors suggest that the depressed mother, because of her own emotional state, fails to respond to her infant's interaction signals, and this results in poorly coordinated interactions, causing the infant to experience consistent negative affect. For a time, the infant may persist in attempting to repair the interactions, but, with each repetition of his or her failure, the infant turns more quickly to self-directed regulatory behaviors such as sucking and rocking, withdrawal and turning away, in order to cope. These behaviors reduce the infant's sensitivity to the inappropriate emotional feedback provided by the mother, and, eventually, the infant's self-directed behaviors dominate his or her style of interacting with the mother. The authors caution, however, that the child's experience with the depressed mother does not necessarily lead to psychopathology or negative developmental effects. When the infant is able to cope successfully, he or she can maintain self-regulation and interactive regulation simultaneously. But when these twin achievements are not possible, self-regulation becomes a predominant goal, and psychopathology is a possible result.

In the second chapter, Garrison and Earls review the literature on various studies, all of which have found a significant relationship between affective disturbance in the mother and detrimental outcomes in the child—despite the studies' divergent ways of measuring and defining maternal depression and its outcomes. The epidemiological data suggest a maternal depression prevalence rate of 12 to 20 percent for mothers of infants and preschoolers, and the authors highlight a number of risk factors that can lead to such depression. These factors include variables such as being the mother of a preschool child, a handicapped or high-risk child, or a temperamental child, and situational variables such as lack of social support and early separation from the child.

The authors conclude their review with a number of suggestions:

First, theoretical models of psychopathology will need to include such variables as marital quality, sociodemographic indexes (especially family composition), parent and child characteristics, and the levels of acute and chronic stress in family life. Second, there is a great need for more sensitive and sophisticated measures of maternal depressive symptomatology. Such measures must define more specific aspects of caretaking behavior that may indicate functional impairment in mother-child interactions. Third, there is a need for better measures of disorders in children, especially children aged birth through three years of age. Researchers should attempt to relate specific forms of child disorder to maternal depression by multidimensional methods of describing child behavior and dysfunction. Fourth, additional longitudinal studies are needed. Finally, researchers need to study the young child's perceptions of the self and others as well as overt behavioral symptoms in order to further our understanding of how maternal depression during the first years of life affects the child's developing sense about the self in the external world.

In the third chapter, Cohn, Matias, Tronick, Connell, and Lyons-Ruth present data on face-to-face interactions of depressed mothers with their infants. The authors' review of the literature suggests that infants and young children of depressed mothers are at increased risk for developmental problems ranging from disturbances in the regulation of affect, to the inability to achieve secure attachment and other social and emotional behaviors, to poor performance on measures of intellectual ability and academic achievement. Face-to-face interactions are a primary way in which behavior and personality disorders may be transmitted from parent to infant.

The authors describe four types of depressed mothers in face-to-face mother-infant interactions: those who appear to be disengaged, those who are intrusive, a mixed group (those showing low proportions of positive expression but high rates of attention-seeking behavior), and a fourth group of positive mothers who engage their infants in active play. Thus, a unique finding of this study is that depressed mothers are not uniformly withdrawn and restricted in their range of emotional expression, as is typically reported in the literature. In the authors' study, the sad, withdrawn picture of maternal depression was noted in some mothers, but others became highly intrusive and were likely to express anger toward their baby. Of interest was that mothers who were intrusive during face-to-face interactions tended to remain distant from their infants during unstructured observations. The authors suggest that depressed mothers, especially those who feel hostile, may cope by limiting the kinds of contact they have and in particular by limiting play interactions. Within limits, this may be adaptive for both the mother and the infant.

In the fourth chapter, Field presents studies suggesting that maternal deprivation may predispose the infant to chronic depression and that the effects of early separations from the mother may provide a model for reactive depression. Primate studies, as well as a study on prolonged separations of human infants, suggest that there is a biphasic response to separation, with a period of agitation followed by a period of depression. The human infants who were separated from their mothers during the mother's hospitalization for the birth of a sibling appeared agitated by the separation; their agitation was by manifested by increased activity level, fussiness, heart rate, night wakings, and nighttime crying. Followng the mother's return, the infants showed decreases in positive affect, activity level, heart rate, and active sleep—symptoms of reactive depression. Field proposes that the primate and human infants may become agitated during separation from the mother due to the loss of an important source of stimulation and arousal modulation. The emergence of depression may be a homeostatic mechanism offsetting the agitation that has occurred due to the absence of effective arousal modulation, or it may result from inadequate amounts of stimulation from the mother upon her return.

Field also presents data from studies on postpartum-depressed mothers and their infants. In these studies, the behavior of the infants appears to "mirror" the behavior of their mothers, suggesting that, by experiencing frequent lack of control during early interactions, the infants may have developed a passive-coping, depressed style of interacting. Their depressed mood persists across interactions and may be a well-established defensive posture. Whether the depressed affect of these infants has resulted from mirroring of their mothers' behaviors, from minimal stimulation provided by the mothers, or from self-regulating the negative affect generated during the interaction is an empirical question.

In the final chapter, Lyons-Ruth, Zoll, Connell, and Grunebaum present data on a sample of mothers and infants who were referred to a clinical infant-intervention service because of a poor mother-infant relationship and economic and social stressors within the family. Maternal depression assessed at the beginning and end of the study was remarkably stable in this low-income sample. As compared to a community group, significantly more mothers in the high-risk group were depressed. Observation of their interactions suggests that increasing maternal depression was associated with increased maternal Covert Hostility, increase Interfering Manipulation, and Flatness of Affect during their interactions with their infants. As in the study described in Chapter Three, several mothers appeared angry and controlling toward their children rather than passive and withdrawn. Of interest were data on some mothers who scored zero on the self-report of depressive symptoms. These mothers were rated particularly high on Covert Hostility and Interfering Manipulation, indicating potential denial. Maternal depression was also significantly related to infants' scores on the Bayley Scales at one year of age. The mothers' intelligence quotients (IQs), together with the severity of maternal depression, accounted for 31 percent of the variance. Despite the significant relationships between maternal depression and maternal behavior and between maternal depression and infant development, maternal depression showed no linear relation to infant attachment behavior.

The reviews of the literature and the recent data presented in this volume appear to suggest, then, that maternal depression has generally negative effects on infant and early childhood development. The exact nature of this relationship is not yet understood, and the models, the research methodology, and the results of these investigators suggest directions for future research. The investigators appear to have responded to the mandate issued by Garrison and Earls for measures that capture both functional impairment in mother-child interactions and more specific aspects of caretaking behavior. They also have attempted to relate specific forms of child disorder to maternal depression by multidimensional methods of describing child behavior and dysfunction. In this way, the laboratory research described in this volume provides a basis for methods that will have clinical utility in the very near future.

Edward Z. Tronick
Tiffany Field
Editors

Edward Z. Tronick is professor of psychology at the University of Massachusetts, Amherst. His research has focused on the social development of the young child in the United States and other countries.

Tiffany Field is professor of pediatrics and psychology at the Mailman Center for Child Development, University of Miami Medical School. Her research has focused on affective development and disorders in infants and young children.

The infants' experience with a depressed mother does not necessarily lead to psychopathology.

The Transmission of Maternal Disturbance to the Infant

Edward Z. Tronick, Andrew F. Gianino, Jr.

How is it that an infant of a depressed mother often becomes sad and withdrawn? Does the mother somehow give her infant some of her depression, as if she were feeding it to him or her? Does the infant imitate or mirror the mother's emotions, becoming sad because she is sad? Does the mother's emotional mood disturb the infant as he or she tries to deal with her? Answers to these questions require an understanding of the normal relationship between maternal emotions and behavior and the development of infant emotions and behavior; asking why an infant may become sad when the mother is sad is no different than asking why an infant may become happy when the mother is happy.

The Mutual Regulation Model

We have developed the Mutual Regulation Model (MRM) (Gianino and Tronick, 1985; Tronick and Gianino, 1986) to describe the infant's dual task of regulating simultaneously his or her internal emotional state

---

This report was supported by grants from the National Science Foundation (BHS8506987) and the National Institute of Mental Health (RO3 MH 40681).

E. Z. Tronick, T. Field (eds.). *Maternal Depression and Infant Disturbance.*
New Directions for Child Development, no. 34. San Francisco: Jossey-Bass, Winter 1986.

and his or her engagement with the external environment. These regulatory functions are inextricably related because emotions provide the motivation for and help to organize the infant's actions on the external environment.

A distressed infant, for example, will be unable to maintain an organized engagement with a person or an object because of his or her disorganizing emotional state. Similarly, it is unlikely that a sad (or angry) infant will be motivated to play with an object or a person, while an interested (or happy) infant probably will be motivated to engage in such forms of play. Thus, emotions are an internal aspect of the infant's activities.

Self-Regulation. Regulation of an appropriate emotional state is not an easy task for the infant. Disruptions to the infant's emotional state come from both inside and outside. They are produced by physiological states such as hunger, conflicting infant goals, too much or too little stimulation, a mismatch of the infant's expectations and the external outcome, too large a discrepancy between the infant's internal schema and the external event, and the like. In the face of these difficulties, the infant can utilize his or her self-directed regulatory behaviors in order to modify internal and external sources of disruption. One set of such behaviors regulates the infant's emotional state by decreasing the infant's engagement with the external environment and by substituting self-stimulating behaviors. These include all forms of self-comfort, such as sucking and rocking, as well as behaviors that decrease the infant's perceptual receptivity, such as withdrawal and turning away. All of these behaviors are accompanied by emotions expressed through face, voice, gesture, and posture.

These self-directed, regulatory capacities are under the infant's control and can be exercised without external support. However, they are not sufficient for the infant to succeed fully at the regulatory task; they are too immature, too limited, too poorly organized and coordinated for the task. The infant requires additional regulatory capacities in order to cope with disruptions of his or her emotional state. This additional capacity is provided to the infant by the mother. The mother reads her infant's self-directed behaviors as a message calling upon her to aid in his or her regulatory efforts. When the mother accurately reads the message conveyed by the infant's self-regulatory behaviors and responds appropriately, she makes the infant's regulatory task easier and enables him or her to self-regulate. For example, a mother seeing her infant rocking and looking dull when engaged with a complex object, such as moving a noisy mobile, may pick the infant up and gently sing to him or her. These maternal regulatory behaviors reduce the stimulation and enable the infant to control the disruption caused by overstimulation from the object. If the mother does not respond, the infant's regulatory efforts may fail, and the child may become disorganized.

Other-Directed Regulation. Paradoxically, the mother's own interactive behavior is a common source of disruption to the infant's emotional state. The mother-child interaction can be characterized as a dyadic system in which the infant and mother attempt to achieve the culturally valued goal of a shared positive emotional state. The infant utilizes other-directed regulatory behaviors, primarily emotional displays, to regulate the mother's behavior. These other-directed behaviors convey the infant's evaluation of the mother's behavior and tell her to continue or to change what she is doing. Infant smiles, for example, signal to the mother that she should continue what she is doing, whereas frowns indicate that the infant does not like what she is doing and that she should change her behavior. When the mother responds appropriately to her infant's other-directed regulatory displays, the infant is able to maintain both self-regulation and regulation of the interaction, and positive emotions are generated. When the mother fails to respond, the infant's regulatory efforts are unsuccessful, and negative emotions are generated. These other-directed regulatory displays, like the self-directed regulatory behaviors, indicate the infant's emotional state. However, unlike the self-directed regulatory behaviors, which decrease the infant's engagement with the external environment, these other-directed behaviors maintain the infant's engagement.

The Mother's Role in Regulation. The mother's behavior has a powerful influence on the infant's emotional state. The infant's regulatory capacity involves the mother because a part of that capacity is a feedback loop that passes through the mother. When the feedback provided by the mother is appropriate to the infant's self- or other-directed regulatory behaviors, she provides the infant with the regulatory capacity that the child lacks, enabling him or her to regulate his or her state successfully. Thus, the infant's regulatory system is fundamentally a dyadic system, dependent on both infant and mother.

Consider early infant reaching as an example from a domain other than social development. A young infant is not able to reach for an object in part because he or she is not yet able to regulate posture, arms, and hands in a coordinated fashion. This lack of sufficient regulatory capacity does not prevent the infant from having the goal of grasping an object, although being unable to achieve this goal is likely to cause distress or anger. But the infant is not without other resources. He or she can signal this goal by looking at an object, making awkward attempts to reach for it, and by fussing. A sensitive caretaker can respond to this signal and help the infant to accomplish the goal—by supporting the infant's posture, by bringing the object closer, and by other actions. These caretaker responses serve as an external segment of the infant's regulatory capacities. They reduce the regulatory demands on the infant and enable him or her to make effective reaches.

The Impact of Mother-Infant Interactions

The normal interaction of an infant and mother has periods of time that are well regulated. The mother responds appropriately to the infant's signals, and the infant experiences positive affect. There are also times when there are interactive errors—for example, when the infant signals "let's play" (by smiling) but the mother fails to respond, or when the mother signals "let's play" but the infant signals "no, I need to stay quiet" (by turning away or becoming glassy eyed). In an ongoing study, we found that the interaction was well coordinated about 3 percent of the time when the infant was three, six, and nine months of age and was discoordinated 70 percent of the time. But we also found that 34 percent of these interactive errors were subsequently repaired during the next step of the interaction, producing a well-coordinated state. Thus, the normal interaction is not always well regulated; rather, it moves from poorly regulated to well regulated states and back again on a frequent basis. Furthermore, these changes in interactive state bring about changes in the infant's emotional state.

We hypothesized that the infant's experience with reparation of the interaction, from a poorly regulated to a well-regulated state, has several positive developmental effects. It allows the infant to elaborate his or her regulatory capacities and to become more skillful in utilizing them. Furthermore, to the extent that this experience of reparation is a consistent and regular feature of the mother-infant interactions, the infant will develop a representation of his or her interaction with the mother as generally well regulated and reparable. He or she will also develop an affective core that is positive, with clearer boundaries between self and others. The infant will then apply this representation of other and self to guide his or her interactions with other partners; that is, it will, in part, structure his or her performance and emotional state when dealing with others.

To evaluate these hypotheses, we had the infant confront the mother when she did not provide him or her with any of her usual regulatory behaviors. We instructed her to remain emotionally expressionless and unresponsive by remaining still-faced while sitting face to face with the infant. Typically, infants responded to this first by attempting to signal the mother. After failing repeatedly in their attempts, many infants turned toward self-directed regulatory behaviors to control the negative emotion they were experiencing.

More specifically, we found that the infants who experienced more repairs during the normal interaction directed more signals toward the mother when she was acting unresponsive and persisted longer in trying to reinstate a normal interaction. We saw this as indicating that they had the clearest representation of the interaction as reparable and of themselves as effective. Infants who had experienced fewer repairs in the normal interaction were more likely to turn away from their mothers and to get distressed and sad. Their reaction suggests that they represented the normal interaction as not being easily reparable and themselves as not being very effective in repairing it. Furthermore, we found stability in the infant's regulatory behaviors. Six-month-old infants demonstrated individual stability in their tendency to use signaling and self-comforting behaviors when they confronted their mother in the still-face posture at two occasions, in visits a week apart. We believe that these infants had developed a regulatory style, an internal representation of their interactive history, based on their experience in the normal interaction.

The Depressed Mother and Infant Regulation

Now we may ask our opening question again: How is it that an infant of a depressed mother comes to be disturbed? From the perspective of the Mutual Regulation Model, we can give the following answer: The depressed mother, because of her own emotional state, fails to respond to her infant's other-directed regulatory signals and thus fails to provide the infant with appropriate regulatory help. This results in poorly coodinated interactions, causing the infant to experience negative affect consistently and repeatedly. For a time, the infant may persist in attempting to repair the interactions, but, with each repetition of his or her failure, he or she more quickly turns to self-directed regulatory behaviors in order to cope with the negative affect generated by the interaction. The infant turns inward, away from social engagement, and increasingly utilizes self-directed regulatory behaviors that reduce his sensitivity to the inappropriate emotional feedback provided by the mother.

Eventually, the infant's cumulation of interactive experience with the depressed mother—and, in particular, the continued "success" his or her self-directed behaviors in reducing the intensity and acuteness of the negative affect—have a structural effect. The infant's self-directed behaviors will then dominate his or her style of interacting with the mother. In addition, the infant will develop a representation of self as ineffective and of the mother as unreliable. Once this representation becomes established, the infant utilizes it to guide his or her interactions with others, distorting those interactions as well.

Thus, the affective disturbance seen in infants of depressed mothers is not the result of mirroring or imitation, or of the mother somehow "feeding" her affect to her infant. Rather, it is the result of the infant's normal regulatory capacities becoming increasingly narrowly deployed in a self-regulatory fashion in the face of the mother's failure to play her normal external regulatory role.

This account pertains to the relatively young infant during the first months of life. With development, the normal infant's capacity to regulate his or her own emotional state increases, and the need for the supplemental regulatory capacity provided by the mother decreases. But, as the infant becomes older, he or she moves on to new, more complex and demanding tasks, such as playing with an object and a person at the same time, or interacting with persons less familiar than the mother, or playing with peers. These tasks place new demands on the infant's ability to be attentive and curious and to remain organized and focused. These self-regulatory demands require supplementation with new forms of regulatory capacities from the mother and others. For example, the mother can begin to use language to aid the infant's attempt to self-regulate while he or she is engaging the environment.

In the case of the depressed mother, we can expect that the older infant will also develop self-regulatory behaviors that minimize the negative emotions experienced with her. These behaviors may be different than those employed by the younger infant; for instance, rather than decreasing perceptual sensitivity to the surroundings (as evidenced in the child who looks dull), the older child can leave the scene, making a strategic withdrawal. But, whatever form the behavior may take with an older child, it still remains a way of controlling negative emotions and anxiety.

Two cautionary notes are in order: First, a child's experience with a depressed mother does not necessarily lead to psychopathology or negative developmental effects. Some effects may be positive. For example, an infant of a depressed mother may become exceedingly sensitive to the mother's emotional state in order to read her better and to regulate the interaction better. This sensitivity may be useful to the child in interactions with others. Relatedly, experience with a depressed mother is likely to have quite different effects on the infant at different points in his or her development. For example, maternal depression during the first months may have little effect on the infant if it does not interfere with the development of the infant's capacity to regulate his or her physiological states of sleep and hunger. On the other hand, experience with a depressed mother when the infant is one year old and just beginning to walk and explore the environment may be particularly detrimental to the development of autonomy if he or she does not receive appropriate regulatory support from the mother.

Second, many factors other than the infant's interactive experiences with the mother affect the course of the infant's development. Even a partial list would include the infant's temperament, genetic predispositions, the social support available to both infant and mother, the infant's other interactive experiences, and the family structure. Thus, while we are hypothesizing that the process of mutual regulation, and the infant's experience with reparation in particular, is a central aspect of the infant's development, we are not contending that it is the only aspect.

Conclusion

From this perspective, the pathways to normalcy or psychopathology appear as part of the same developmental process. The central event of the process is the interactive error. The critical developmental experience has to do with whether or not the infant's regulatory behaviors successfully repair the error and maintain or fail to maintain self-regulation. We see no single traumatic juncture separating these pathways—only the infant's slowly accumulated and eventually internalized experience. When the infant is able to cope successfully, he or she can maintain self- and interactive regulation simultaneously. When these twin achievements are not possible, self-regulation becomes the predominant goal and psychopathology a possible result.

References

Gianino, A., and Tronick, E. "The Mutual Regulation Model: The Infant's Self and Interactive Regulation and Coping and Defensive Capacities." In R. Field, P. McCabe, and N. Schneiderman (eds.), *Stress and Coping*. Hillsdale, N.J.: Erlbaum, 1985.

Tronick, E. Z., and Gianino, A. "Interactive Mismatch and Repair: Challenges to Infant Coping." *Zero to Three*, 1986, 1-6.

Edward Z. Tronick is professor of psychology at the University of Massachusetts, Amherst. His research has focused on the social development of the young child in the United States and other countries.

Andrew F. Gianino, Jr., is a clinical child psychologist and the director of a National Science Foundation project on the infant's capacity to cope with interpersonal stress.

Epidemiological studies of depressive symptoms in mothers and possible outcomes for their children offer a glimpse of these phenomena in the general population that cannot be found in clinical studies.

Epidemiological Perspectives on Maternal Depression and the Young Child

William T. Garrison, Felton J. Earls

Several separate lines of research and clinical inquiry reveal interesting and useful patterns that are relevant to our understanding of maternal depression and its putative role in the development of child psychopathology. These research approaches have included a number of clinical studies of the offspring of psychiatrically depressed parents (Beardslee and others, 1983; Weissman and others, 1984; Welner and others, 1977), epidemiological surveys of depression and its correlates in women during the childbearing years (Richman, 1978; Bromet and Cornely, 1984; Werner and Smith, 1981; Moss and Lewis, 1977; Brown and others, 1975), and interaction analyses of high-risk and normal mother-infant dyads (Field, 1980; Als and others, 1979; Cohn and Tronick, 1983; Lewis and Schaeffer, 1981). Findings across this literature strongly suggest a significant relationship between affective disturbance in the mother and detrimental outcomes in the child, despite the studies' rather divergent ways of measuring and defining maternal depression and its outcomes in infants and young children.

This chapter acquaints the reader with one specific approach to the question of maternal depression and its impact on infant development. This approach is derived from epidemiological studies on the prevalence of maternal depression in the general population and the social etiology of behavioral and psychiatric disorder in early childhood. First, we will describe some of these epidemiological studies and consider the data on the problem of maternal depression in women with children generally under the age of four years. (Outcome data will be examined in the children of depressed mothers up to seven years of age.) Then we will report on our work in Martha's Vineyard and use our experience to point out avenues of much-needed further research.

This chapter differs from others in this volume in that our focus, in terms of dysfunction in the child, is primarily on children after the age of three years. The studies we will discuss have been concerned with estimating the prevalence and etiology of identifiable disorder using techniques designed for the young child. Measures of dysfunction prior to the age of three are still, in our view, in need of further development and validation. Thus, this chapter will delineate the longer-term effects of depressive patterns in mothers of infants and toddlers; in so doing, it may help to frame the other studies in this volume.

Epidemiology and the Study of Childhood Disorders

Goals of the Epidemiological Survey. The primary goals of an epidemiological survey, whether focused on social, physical, or psychological phenomena, are to estimate the prevalence of certain disorders or conditions and to identify factors that appear to correlate with such disorders. Recently, these studies have also sought to pose questions concerning causality and etiology in longitudinal surveys of larger samples. The epidemiologist must seek always to achieve a balance between (1) ensuring valid measures with representative samples of the general population and (2) avoiding reduction to a superficial investigation of the phenomenon of interest.

Findings on the Prevalence of Childhood Disorders. Most epidemiological studies of childhood disorders have used samples taken from children aged six through eighteen years. Reasons for this range from the assumption that true psychiatric disorder is much more likely to manifest itself with increasing age to the various obstacles involved in accessing large representative samples of preschool-aged children and the lack of validated measures or concepts of disorder in these younger children.

In recent years, however, several attempts have been made to expand the epidemiological approach to children under age six and their families. Techniques found to be useful in the longer tradition of medical and demographic epidemiology have been applied to the special area of early childhood disorder with its correlates and etiology. These studies have also borrowed from clinical research on the manifestation of psychological dysfunction in the preschool child.

Previous studies have suggested that between 15 and 20 percent of the general population manifests behavioral and/or psychiatric symptoms at moderate to marked levels. Conservative estimates would indicate that about 12 percent of the school-aged child population currently has a diagnosable psychiatric disorder, using the nosology of the Diagnostic and Statistical Manual of the American Psychiatric Association (DSM-III).

For children under six years of age, fewer data are available. First, only a handful of studies have been completed, and, second, attempts to develop more adequate diagnostic classification schemes for these children are a relatively recent development. Most studies have employed symptom inventories covering an array of common behavior problems with an additive approach that combines numbers of symptoms and, in some studies, frequency of occurrence. In the better studies, such inventories are followed by clinical assessment of the children or case protocols of identified children. Clinical judges have also been used to ascertain cutoffs for disordered groups and, in some cases, to detect atypical psychiatric presentation in a more qualitative fashion. The bulk of this work suggests that a prevalence between 8 and 14 percent characterizes the rate of psychiatric disorder in preschool-aged children across various samples in the Western Hemisphere. The deficiencies we have noted, however, serve to qualify such conclusions.

Prevalence and Correlates of Maternal Depression

Prevalence Rates. The range in prevalence rates of maternal depression, especially as these rates relate to the mother with a child aged three years and under, is strongly influenced by both sample and method characteristics. Differences have been noted to occur as a function of cultural and subcultural context, social class, and divergent classification schemes for identifying and categorizing depressive phenomena. For example, in narrowly defined subgroups of the general population, rates of depressive phenomena in women have ranged from 40 to 80 percent. This range of rates has been observed in samples of women in specialized health settings or who are defined at elevated risk for psychiatric disorders as a function of personal history, current life conditions, and an array of miscellaneous stress conditions. For example, single mothers and, especially, black female heads of household (Orr and James, 1984; Belle, 1982; Eaton and Kessler, 1981) have been found to exhibit very high rates of depressive symptoms (up to 80 percent). Also, maternal depressed mood and accompanying symptomatology have long been recognized as more likely within the first three months following the birth of a child (Elliot and others, 1983; Yalom and others, 1968).

The range of prevalence rates of maternal depression reported across epidemiological or quasi-epidemiological studies has been from 25 to over

50 percent in the United Kingdom (Ghodsian and others, 1984; Richman and others, 1975; Richman, 1977; Moss and Lewis, 1977); generally lower rates have been reported in the United States, from 12 to 20 percent (Bromet and Cornely, 1984; Bromet and others, 1982; Garrison and Earls, 1983a). These rates derive specifically from studies of mothers with very young children (between ages four months and five years). Cultural factors are often mentioned as a chief cause for observed differences in rates, but we would also point to methodological variations as an important factor. First of all, each study has usually chosen a single and often unique means of assessing depression. Some studies have used simple inventories of symptoms judged to be relevant to depression, with numbers of symptoms ranging from five to over twenty-five individual items. Others have used interview schedules based upon standardized systems such as the Research Diagnostic Criteria (Spitzer and others, 1977), the Feighner criteria (Feighner and others, 1972), the International Classification and Diagnostic System of the World Health Organization (ICD-9), and DSM-III.

Second, there has been only limited attention to other psychiatric disorders that often include depressive symptoms in the clinical presentation. In other words, some investigations have assumed that the women identified through survey screening would all be diagnosed with a depressive disorder of some type, when in actuality many of these women would probably not meet criteria for disorders other than clinical depression.

To illustrate these points, we will look at data from the Epidemiologic Catchment Area (ECA) survey recently completed in the metropolitan St. Louis area in the United States. This survey is one of five situated in major U.S. urban and suburban areas; all seek to ascertain the prevalence rates of various psychiatric disorders in representative and stratified samples.

Table 1 displays a detailed breakdown of various psychiatric conditions that can include depressive symptoms to varying degrees. These data are separated for women on the basis of having a child under the age of six in the home. The lifetime diagnosis rate was approximately 22 percent for these women. There was only one significant difference as a function of having a young child in the home, and this difference was not found in depression itself. These women were interviewed using a schedule keyed to the DSM-III approach. The current diagnosis rate was found to be approximately 14 percent with no differences due to the presence of preschool-aged children. This finding, which awaits replication in other samples, is based upon a highly representative sample of women from a heterogeneous population; it demonstrates that women who describe depressive disturbances on symptom inventories (as used in other studies discussed in this chapter) would not all meet stricter criteria for clinical depression within a psychiatric nosology. It also suggests that the effect of younger children on mothers is not a predictive of psychiatric disorder, as previously thought.

Table 1. Association of Having Young Children
with Psychiatric Diagnosis in Women (Age Adjusted)

	Lifetime Diagnosis (%)		Current Symptoms (%)	
	Child<6 (391)	No Child<6 (1,140)	Child<6 (391)	No Child<6 (1,140)
Depressive episode	5.6	7.9	3.7	3.2
Dysthymia	2.9	2.7	2.6	1.1
Alcohol abuse/dependence	3.1	6.2	1.5	3.4
Drug abuse/dependence	4.4	6.6	2.0	3.9
Antisocial personality	1.8	1.6	1.8	1.6
Phobia	13.9[a]	9.1[a]	8.4	6.5
Obsessive-compulsive disorder	2.3	1.9	0.4	1.1
Any diagnosis	22.2	22.8	14.2	14.3

[a] $p \leq .05$

Source: Earls, Sussman, and Robins, 1986.

These data are much in line with findings from another sample of mothers with very young children in the United States. Bromet and Cornely (1984) found that increments in depressive symptoms did occur in the women in their sample following the birth of a child, but overall they found that depression in these women appeared more intimately associated to marital conflict than to child rearing itself. This study also found prevalence rates that are in line with the figures of psychiatric disorder found in the St. Louis ECA study. The average age of children of the mothers in Bromet and Cornely's survey was three years, yet the mothers' reported prevalence rates are not more than 3 to 8 percentage points higher than those observed in the ECA data. Again, remember that we are speaking of diagnosable psychiatric disorders and not broad symptomatic descriptions of depressive experiences or depressive episodes. Studies we will discuss later in this chapter indicate that rates of *subclinical* forms of affective disturbance, as compared to psychiatric disturbance in general, do appear to be occurring at higher rates in mothers with very young children.

Correlates. Several epidemiological surveys that have investigated childhood disorders have reported on factors observed to correlate with these phenomena. Most prominent among such factors have been quality of marriage and level of marriage conflict, social and demographic indexes of various types, broader family and school factors, and the occurrence of stressful events in family and child life (Links, 1983; Garrison and Earls,

1983b). A recurrent finding of the literature concerned with childhood disorders has involved the identification of higher rates of depressive symptoms in the mothers of disordered children. Ironically, these children are most often identified as having disorders solely (or heavily) on the basis of behavioral reports from the mothers themselves. This approach has led to confusion and controversy concerning both the validity of such reports and the causal connection, if any, between the two variables (Achenbach, 1980). Despite this controversy, the finding of a moderately strong correlation between the presence or absence of child disorder and depressive symptoms in the mother remains relatively robust.

Across clinical and epidemiological studies, specific conditions and events have been correlated, in quantitative and/or qualitative fashion, with maternal depressive symptoms. These include aspects of social support (Weintraub and Wolf, 1983; Garrison and Earls, 1983b), early separation from child (Seashore and others, 1973; Leifer and others, 1972), failure-to-thrive syndrome (Als and others, 1976), and medical problems during the prenatal through postnatal period (Kaplan and Mason, 1960; Beckwith and Cohen, 1978; Field, 1979; Goldberg, 1979). In addition, some studies have indicated that the occurrence of depressive symptoms (but not necessarily of psychiatric disorder) is more likely in mothers of preschool-aged children (Richman, 1978; Kendall and others, 1976; Moss and Lewis, 1977). This finding has been attributed to a multitude of factors that characterize this period in the child-rearing years and that include intensified economic and marital strains, adaptation to parenthood, and interactional contributions of the child (Brown and Harris, 1978; Earls, 1981). Despite considerable differences in the manner in which investigators have measured these factors and their relationship to maternal depression, most studies have continued to suggest powerful etiological effects, especially from combinations of key correlates. Unfortunately, only a few studies have been longitudinal in nature, and even these have been limited in their ability to make more definitive statements regarding the exact nature of such an etiology.

Directly related to the observed relationship between childhood behavioral disorders and maternal depression has been the work examining temperamental characteristics in infants and toddlers. Temperament has been hypothesized by many to underlie an array of behavioral and interactional disturbances in children's lives (Thomas and Chess, 1980; Bates, 1980). Several studies have specifically linked emotional upset in the mother, typically involving anxiety or depressive reactions, with temperament constellations of various kinds in the child. For example, Thomas and Chess (1977, 1984) have written extensively on the dynamic effects of poor temperamental "fit" between mother and an infant whom they classify as "difficult." Such a child has been viewed as manifesting a consistent temperamental pattern of negative mood, poor adaptability to change, low rhythmicity or regularity in biological functions, and, in subsequent studies, high intensity of response. This pattern, in turn, is viewed as eliciting certain dysfunctional parenting responses from the caretaker—responses that often include emotional upset. Other researchers concerned with infant or toddler temperament and its role in the emotional status of the mother have reported similar findings with some variation as a function of methods, sample composition, and theoretical perspective (Plomin, 1982).

Longitudinal Studies

Several epidemiological or quasi-epidemiological studies of families with young children have special relevance to this chapter. The researchers who have directed these studies have come from somewhat different perspectives and have therefore applied varying concepts and methods. They all have in common, however, certain advantages that derive from the longitudinal approach.

Let us first consider the valuable work of Naomi Richman and her colleagues in the United Kingdom (Richman, 1977, 1978; Richman and others, 1975, 1982). She has collected population data since the early seventies that have examined the role of maternal depressive symptoms and the factors associated with them in the development of early behavior problems in children. Her samples have been drawn from boroughs of London, England. In one study (Richman and others, 1982) of over 700 three-year-olds randomly selected from the Waltham Forest Family Register, she reported that maternal depression, as measured via a "malaise inventory," occurred in approximately 30 percent of the mothers. Richman's "depressed" mothers were also found to be more likely to lose control in disciplining their child and had more frequently considered leaving their home and child altogether. Most of these depressed mothers—from 48 to 77 percent—had sought some formal assistance in the previous year from their physician (pediatrician or family physician). Richman did not report significant association between maternal depression and social support indexes, but she did find a relationship between depressive symptoms and level of social stress as measured by summing both acute life events and chronic conditions deemed as stress provoking.

Longitudinal follow-up of a representative subsample by Richman and her colleagues (Richman, Stevenson, and Graham, 1982) also revealed interesting findings related to maternal depression and subsequent outcomes in the child. Most importantly, their analyses suggest that ongoing disturbances in family relationships, one of which involves affective dysfunction in the mother, help statistically to predict continuity in child behavior disorders during the preschool to school years. More specifically, maternal emotional state is depicted as a correlated factor in those children who were initially identified as problematic in the preschool period and again at follow-up several years hence. However, because of the lack of specific emphasis in this study on the longitudinal measurement of maternal depression, it is impossible to distinguish true causative effects over time from an ongoing correlational relationship.

Ghodsian and associates (1982, 1984) performed a study involving a sample of firstborns and their mothers in a London borough. Influenced by findings from Richman's work and by earlier studies by Brown and Harris (1978), these researchers sought to chart the natural course of maternal depression, child behavior difficulties, and the associations between these variables across four points in time during early childhood. Mothers and their babies were initially seen four months following the birth of the child and then again when the child was fourteen, twenty-seven, and forty-two months old. Clinical ratings of maternal depression were derived from interviewers with direction from psychiatrists on the research team. Using symptom and interview data, raters judged the mothers as either "depressed," "dubiously depressed," or "normal." The emphasis in these ratings was on the *degree of impairment* caused by the depressive symptoms and not merely on the number or type of symptoms reported.

Wolkind and others (1980) had already reported on the rather high stability of maternal depression over time in this sample, but Ghodsian and his colleagues sought to delineate further the longitudinal association between child behavior difficulties and depression-related impairment in the mothers by providing detailed statistical breakdowns of the data collected across the four study points. They reported that a significant longitudinal relationship existed between behavioral problems identified at twenty-seven and forty-two months following birth and maternal depression detected only at fourteen and twenty-seven months. In addition, behavioral difficulties assessed at fourteen months did not relate to depression prior to that point (that is, at four months), but these difficulties did have a concurrent association with depression. Finally, Ghodsians' study suggested that maternal depression did not appear to derive from the presence of child behavior problems, as some have hypothesized; in their sample, impairment from depression was found prior to the onset of the children's problems.

Ghodsian and his colleagues pointed out some of the limitations of their data but were still able to offer several interesting models of specific etiology that derived from their longitudinal perspective. First, significant relationships among depression in the mother fourteen months after the child's birth and concurrent "overcrowding" conditions combined to predict subsequent child behavior problems at twenty-seven months. Also, the arrival of a sibling prior to the twenty-seven month follow-up point appeared to potentiate the effects of maternal depression detected at fourteen months on the development of child problems later on. Depressed mothers in this sample were more likely to use physical punishment with their children, as had been observed in Richman's study (1978). Ghodsian and his colleagues also reported that maternal depression at twenty-seven months was more closely associated with child behavior difficulties if the mother was at home and not in the work force during the period between fourteen and twenty-seven months after the child's birth.

The design and general approach of this study, especially in its longitudinal emphasis on assessing the impairment associated with depressive symptomatology and not merely symptoms alone, serves as an excellent example of the direction work in this area should take. Overreliance on symptom inventories or nosological classification does not allow the investigator to capture the broader range of depressive phenomena, especially in more heterogeneous samples of the general population. Research must begin to translate assessments of maternal depression into multiple elements including, but not limited to, overall level of functional impairment, duration of impairment, and specific constellations of symptoms that may have greater or lesser relative effects on the infant or young child. For example, we should be able to differentiate between a mother who is characterized by predominantly low self-esteem versus the mother who is afflicted with an array of moderate sleep, appetite, and drive disturbances.

Ghodsian and others' study did not find longer-term effects of the maternal depression measured at four months following the birth of the child. This fact merits closer scrutiny. Numerous clinical studies of psychiatrically depressed mothers would suggest a much stronger relationship between such early depression and child behavior disturbance, although few of these studies have studied children under the age of six (Beardslee and others, 1983), and these clinically-derived samples are much less heterogeneous. However, both the British and American studies from general population samples do not show such a strong longitudinal relationship, especially in the first two to three years following the birth of the child. Admittedly, all of these studies have not been able to make direct assessments of infants and toddlers using more sophisticated measures to detect behavioral or emotional dysfunction. Therefore, we must await applications of better measures and more longitudinal studies before we draw conclusions about the immediate effects of maternal depression on the very young child.

Michael Lewis and his colleagues (Lewis, Feiring, McGuffog, and Jaskir, 1984) performed a longitudinal study of 113 children who were seen initially at the end of the first year of life and then were seen again at age six. The investigators examined the quality of early attachment relationship to the mothers and the development of subsequent psychopathology (measured by behavior reports from the mother) five years later. Characterizing infant-mother relations in terms of the quality of attachment derives from the theoretical work of Bowlby (1969, 1973) and the Strange-Situation paradigm introduced by Ainsworth and others (1978). Many child development reseachers and theorists have believed that the quality of early attachment, or the social bond between mother and infant, is predictive of subsequent personality and pathology. However, ratings of infant behavior and temperament have not generally held powerful or even moderate predictive significance for subsequent personality development (Beckwith, 1979; Thomas and Chess, 1984). Lewis and Starr (1979) proposed that this relatively weak continuity over time may be more a function of inadequate measures than of the nature of human developments.

Lewis and others (1984) did find that attachment to mother in the child's first year is useful in the prediction of psychopathology for boys but not for girls. This relationship was not found to be a strong one, and the authors concluded that the child is "neither made invulnerable by an early secure attachment nor doomed to psychopathology by an insecure attachment" (p. 123). They went on to suggest that level of life stress and certain family demographic variables (such as birth planning and order) also provide predictive utility in psychopathology for boys in their sample; this finding is consistent with the results of the British studies of preschool-aged children that we have already discussed.

The Lewis and others' study is important in several respects. First, although it did not focus specifically on maternal depression, it examines what many presume to be an effect of depression in the mother—namely disturbances in mother-child bonding and interaction. Second, its methodology is based on theory to a much larger degree than the methods of other studies we have considered. Third, it attempted to relate mother-infant attachment in the first year to empirically defined dimensions of child psychopathology or behavior derived from state-of-the-art instruments (Achenbach and Edelbrock, 1981) for parent and teacher reports concerning child functioning.

Just as we commented on the need for more detailed assessment of maternal depression, we would also argue for studies that seek to link maternal depression and its correlates to specific forms of child psychopathology, whether they be measured via psychiatric nosologies or empirically derived behavior typologies. For example, Lewis and colleagues reported specific associations over time between subclassifications of attachment and narrowly defined behavioral dimensions. Avoidant males were found to score significantly higher than Secure males on the Schizoid scale of the Child Behavior Profile (Achenbach, 1978). However, the Ambivalent group of boys scored higher on the Depression scale of the profile. These differences are illustrative of the value of more differentiated classification schemes for both mother-infant characteristics and outcome indexes.

A longitudinal study reported by Bates, Maslin, and Frankel (1985) also merits special attention. These investigators followed 120 infants drawn from a general population sample seeing the children at ages six, thirteen, twenty-four, and thirty-six months. Here again the study attempted to examine the role of attachment security in the development of child psychopathology. In this case, the researchers examined a two-and-a-half-year period in early childhood. The study findings indicate that responsive and affectionate mother behavior was followed by secure attachment in the infants, but the predictive power of this relationship was rather limited. The authors also sought to relate attachment security to various temperament characteristics (such as sociability, difficultness, and activity level). They report that temperament was generally unrelated to attachment measures. The study also attempted to construct a multivariate model to explain child psychopathology (defined by the presence of behavior problems) using attachment security, temperament ratings from mothers and observers, and an array of demographic variables. Mother-defined behavior problems in the three-year-olds were best predicted via early mother perceptions of difficult temperament (see Bates, 1980, for an overview of this concept and its controversies). We could argue that the study measured the same thing at both points in time, since considerable overlap probably exists between behavior problem inventories and temperament questionnaires (Garrison and others, 1984). More important, perhaps, was the very low longitudinal association between infant attachment and observers' temperament ratings.

Insofar as mother-infant bonding is influenced by the mental or emotional status of the mother, the longitudinal studies described here suggest that such interaction may not manifest overtly measurable effects during the second and third years of the child's life. The inadequacies of our measures continue to qualify such a conclusion, of course, but, in terms provided by current definitions of psychiatric disorder, such effects have been difficult to pinpoint. The emerging literature on laboratory-based infant and toddler assessments leads us to suspect that more sensitive measures will be forthcoming. We believe that such work will begin to establish a new understanding of the premorbid characteristics of child psychopathology.

The Martha's Vineyard Child Health Survey

Our recently completed study on the island of Martha's Vineyard, Massachusetts, illustrates some additional points (Garrison and Earls, 1983a; Garrison, Earls, and Kindlon, 1984). We attempted to survey a total population sample of families with children born on this island during four separate calendar years. We used a cross-panel, longitudinal design, and our study had several goals: First, we were interested in the prevalence rates of preschool behavior problems in this sample with demonstrated representativeness to the larger U.S. population. We were successful in the initial phase of the survey in obtaining a sample that comprised over 90 percent of the total population. Results from this initial phase of pilot studies, which served to estimate prevalence rates and further develop methods for evaluating behavioral disorders in preschool-aged children, have been presented elsewhere (Earls, 1980a, 1980b).

A second phase was concerned with the application of a particular methodology for examining the multivariate associations among several key variables hypothesized to play a role in the complicated etiology of childhood psychiatric and behavioral disorders. These variables include child temperament characteristics prior to age three years, specified aspects of parental health and life-style, more traditional sociodemographic indexes, and a close examination of the occurrence and timing of stressful life events (Garrison and Earls, 1983a). This last variable was measured using a modified technique originally used by Brown (1974) in the United Kingdom. While this longitudinal study of children from birth to three years of age did not target maternal depression as a primary focus, several of the survey findings are relevant to this topic.

When we analyzed longitudinal data from the first cohort of our survey—a cohort that was comprised of three-year-olds subsequently followed to age six—we noted an intriguing association that emerged as statistically significant. Remember that this population is quite heterogeneous and that, therefore, data analysis at the group level reflects trends in the general population. Maternal depressive ratings provided by interviewers at the time of initial evaluation were longitudinally associated with a rather specific aspect of the child's social perceptions at follow-up. We employed the pictorial version of the Perceived Competence Scale for Young Children, an innovative instrument designed by Susan Harter (1982) and her colleagues at the University of Denver. One dimension identified by Harter involves the child's perceptions of maternal acceptance; other dimensions are concerned with physical, cognitive, and social competence. Maternal depression ratings when the children were three correlated over time with scores on this Maternal Acceptance dimension at a moderately low level ($-.26$, $p < .02$), while another variable, number of siblings, correlated at a somewhat higher level ($-.34$, $p < .01$). Because of the preliminary nature of these data, the heterogeneity of the sample, and our plans to complete analyses on an additional three cohorts of children, we were not prepared to offer an interpretation of these results or make any final statements regarding their meaning. However, we did perform a case-by-case analysis of the protocols for the children who were identified as having mothers with atypically high ratings on maternal depression. These were a relatively small number, of course, but it was interesting to note that over half of these children were found to score exceedingly low in the Maternal Acceptance dimension on Harter's instrument. Since we did not measure affective disturbances in the mother at follow-up, one could argue that mother's depression was ongoing and that we merely captured continued phenomena associated with having a depressed mother concurrently. Still, the finding has increased our interest in the longer-term effects of maternal depression in this population.

Another finding may be relevant both to the course of maternal depressive symptoms and to explanations of observed cohort effects in prevalence rates. Using a rather crude screening inventory of depressive symptoms in our total population sample, we found mothers in one cohort displaying appreciably lower levels of symptoms than mothers in the remaining cohorts. Furthermore, these differences appeared to fluctuate as a function of the particular time of follow-up (see Table 2).

We do not have a good explanation for these differences yet, but we hope that more extensive analyses of other factors (including stressful conditions and life events) will reveal possible sources. We report this pattern in our data to emphasize that researchers must take care in longitudinal studies with regard to the nature of depressive phenomena and to potential cohort effects emanating from sample-specific characteristics, such as sociohistorical and subcultural context.

Summary

Our understanding of the practical outcomes of early maternal depression is currently piecemeal at best. Certain recurrent patterns in the findings of several epidemiological studies strongly suggest, however, that maternal affective dysfunction is significant in the development of child psychopathology. The exact role of the mother's mental and emotional status in this process is quite unclear, as are the specific pathologic outcomes in the child. The studies discussed here have also pointed to the possibility of a multivariate explanation for behavioral and emotional dysfunction in the child. It is evident that theoretic models of psychopathology will need to include such variables as marital quality, sociodemographic indexes (especially family composition), parent and child characteristics, and levels of acute and chronic stress in family life. Mater-

Table 2. Depression Scale Ratings by Age and Cohort

Cohort (Age of Child)	Maternal Depression Rating		
	Marked	Moderate	Mild
01 (24 months)	0%	2%	12%
01 (36 months)	0%	19%	12%
02 (24 months)	8%	18%	6%
02 (24 months)	8%	6%	14%

Note: Marked = four symptoms or more; *moderate* = two or three symptoms; *mild* = one symptom.

nal depressive symptomatology does not appear to have a powerful direct influence on the onset of early child disorder, but it combines with other risk factors to render the particular child vulnerable to pathology.

This overview serves to point out shortcomings in the existing research and also suggests some new directions for investigators interested in the topic. First, there is a great need for more sensitive and sophisticated measures of maternal depressive symptomatology. Such measures must capture functional impairment within the context of mother-child interactions, and they must examine more specific aspects of caretaking behavior. Such an approach will need to take into account various symptom constellations, duration of disturbance, presence or absence of non-depression-related symptoms, the particular effects of affective disturbances in the mother on caretaking routine, access, and utilization of support networks, and individual/family response to life stress.

Second, there is a need for better measures of disorder in children, especially children aged birth through three year years of age. Some of the laboratory research described elsewhere in this volume promises to provide a basis for methods that will have clinical utility in the very near future. It is important that researchers attempt to relate specific forms of child disorder to maternal depression via multidimensional methods of describing child behavior and dysfunction. We feel that the methodology offered by Achenbach and Edelbrock (1980) is a good example of an empirically derived behavior typology with application to both homogeneous and heterogeneous samples of children. Such a typology currently does not exist for children under five years of age; the best alternative available now are measures of temperamental characteristics of the young child.

As is most areas of behavioral research, there is a need for additional longitudinal studies. Specifically, we recommend that researchers begin to address the mediating and causative effects of maternal depressive symptomatology at various intervals of early child development. The study reported by Ghodsian and others (1984) serves as a good example of this approach. We know that affective disturbances in women show a broad range of clinical presentation in terms of symptoms, duration, and impairment of function. Therefore, it is important that we develop methods for characterizing both the natural course of depressive phenomena in mothers and its continuous interaction with other risk variables. In addition, the possible cohort effects that we have noted in the Martha's Vineyard sample lead us to caution other investigators to remain aware of potentially powerful differences in samples—differences that derive from sociohistorical and cultural influences.

Finally, there is a need to study the young child's perceptions of the self and others, as well as overt behavioral symptoms, in order to determine how maternal depression during the first years of life affects the child's developing sense about the self and the external world. For example, subjective data of this kind might be linked to measures of parent-child interaction collected much earlier, during infancy or toddlerhood. In this way, we may come to understand more fully the etiology of emotional disorders in children and to develop a guiding theory that moves beyond simplistic, behavioral explanation or disconfirmable, psychodynamic dogma.

References

Achenbach, T. M. "The Child Behavior Profile, I: Boys Aged 6-11." *Journal of Consulting and Clinical Psychology*, 1978, *46* (3), 478-488.

Achenbach, T. M. "What Is Child Psychiatric Epidemiology the Epidemiology Of?" In F. Earls (ed.), *Studies of Children*. New York: Prodist, 1980.

Achenbach, T. M., and Edelbrock, C. S. "A Typology of Child Behavior Profile Patterns: Distribution and Correlates for Disturbed Children Aged 6-16." *Journal of Abnormal Child Psychology*, 1980, *8*, 441-470.

Achenbach, T. M., and Edelbrock, C. S. "Behavioral Problems and Competencies Reported by Parents of Normal and Disturbed Children Aged 4 Through 14."*Monographs of the Society for Research in Child Development*, 1981, *46* (1), entire issue.

Ainsworth, M.D.S., Blehar, M. C., Waters, E., and Wall, S. *Patterns of Attachment: A Psychological Study of the Strange Situation*. Hillsdale, N.J.: Erlbaum, 1978.

Als, H., Tronick, E. Z., Adamson, L., and Brazelton, B. "The Behavior of the Full-Term Yet Underweight Newborn Infant." *Developmental Medicine and Child Neurology*, 1976, *18*, 590-602.

Als, H., Tronick, E., and Brazelton, T. B. "Analysis of Face-to-Face Interaction in Infant-Adult Dyads." In M. E. Lamb, S. J. Suomi, and G. B. Stephenson (eds.), *Social Interaction Analysis: Methodological Issues*. Madison: University of Wisconsin Press, 1979.

Bates, J. E. "The Concept of Difficult Temperament." *Merrill-Palmer Quarterly*, 1980, *26*, 299-319.

Bates, J. E., Maslin, C. A., and Frankel, K. A. "Attachment Security, Mother-Child Interaction, and Temperament as Predictors of Behavior Problem Ratings at Age Three Years." In I. Bretherton and E. Waters (eds.), *Growing Points of Attachment Theory and Research*. Child Development Monographs, no. 209, *50*. Chicago: Chicago University Press, 1985.

Beardslee, W. R., Bemporad, J., Keller, M. B., and Klerman, G. L. "Children of Parents with Major Affective Disorders: A Review." *American Journal of Psychiatry*, 1983, *140* (7), 825-832.

Beckwith, L. "Prediction of Emotional and Social Behavior." In J. D. Osofsky (ed.), *Handbook of Infant Development*. New York: Wiley, 1979.

Beckwith, L., and Cohen, S. E. "Preterm Birth: Hazardous Obstetrical and Postnatal Events as Related to Caregiver-Infant Behavior." *Infant Behavior and Development*, 1978, *1*, 403-411.

Belle, D. "Introduction." In D. Belle (ed.), *Lives in Stress: Women and Depression*. Beverly Hills, Calif.: Sage, 1982.

Bowlby, J. *Attachment and Loss, Vol. I: Attachment*. New York: Basic, 1969.

Bowlby, J. *Attachment and Loss, Vol. II: Separation: Anxiety and Anger*. New York: Basic, 1973.

Bromet, E., and Cornely, M.P.H. "Correlates of Depression in Mothers of Young Children." *Journal of the American Academy of Child Psychiatry*, 1984, *23* (3), 335-342.

Bromet, E., Solomon, Z., Dunn, L., and Nicklas, N. "Affective Disorders in Mothers of Young Children." *British Journal of Psychiatry*, 1982, *140*, 30-36.

Brown, G. W. "Meaning, Measurement, and Stressful Life Events." In B. Dohrewend and B. Dohrewend (eds.), *Stressful Life Events: Their Nature and Effects*. New York: Wiley-Interscience, 1974.

Brown, G. W., Bhrolchain, M. N., and Harris, T. "Social Class and Psychiatric Disturbance Among Women in an Urban Population." *Sociology*, 1975, *9*, 225-254.

Brown, G. W., and Harris, T. *Social Origins of Depression*. London: Tavistock, 1978.

Cohn, J. F., and Tronick, E. Z. "Three-Month-Old Infants' Reaction to Simulated Maternal Depression." *Child Development*, 1983, *54*, 185-193.

Earls, F. J. "The Prevalence of Behavior Problems in Three-Year-Old Children: A Cross-National Replication." *Archives of General Psychiatry*, 1980a, *37*, 1153-1157.

Earls, F. J. "The Prevalence of Behavior Problems in Three-Year-Old Children: Comparison of the Reports of Mothers and Fathers." *Journal of the American Academy of Child Psychiatry*, 1980b, *19*, 439-452.

Earls, F. J. "Temperamental Characteristics and Behavior Problems in Three-Year-Old Children." *Journal of Nervous and Mental Disease*, 1981, *169*, 367-373.

Earls, F. J., Sussman, M., and Robins, L. Unpublished data. St. Louis, Mo.: Washington University School of Medicine, 1986.

Eaton, W. W., and Kessler, I. G. "Rates of Symptoms of Depression in a National Sample." *American Journal of Epidemiology*, 1981, *114*, 528-538.

Elliot, S. A., Rugg, A. J., Watson, J. P., and others. "Mood Changes During Pregnancy and After the Birth of the Child." *British Journal of Clinical Psychology*, 1983, *22*, 295-308.

Feighner, J. P., Robins, E., Guze, S. B., Woodruff, R. A., Winokur, G., and Muñoz, R. "Diagnostic Criteria for Use in Psychiatric Research." *Archives of General Psychiatry*, 1972, *26*, 57-63.

Field, T. "Interaction Patterns of High-Risk and Normal Infants." In T. Field, A. Sostek, S. Goldburg, and H. Shuman (eds.), *Infants Born at Risk*. New York: Spectrum, 1979.

Field, T. "Interaction of High-Risk Infants: Quantitative and Qualitative Differences." In D. B. Swain, R. C. Hawkins, L. O. Walker, and J. Penticuff (eds.), *Exceptional Infant: Psychosocial Risks in Infant-Environment Transactions*. New York: Brunner/Mazel, 1980.

Garrison, W. T., and Earls, F. J. "Life Events and Social Support in Families with a Preschool-Aged Child: Methods and Preliminary Findings." *Comprehensive Psychiatry*, 1983a, *24*, 439-452.

Garrison, W. T., and Earls, F. J. "Stress in Family Life, Maternal Depression, and Competence Outcomes in the Young Child: A Longitudinal Analysis." Paper presented at the annual meeting of the American Academy of Child Psychiatry, San Francisco, California, October 26-30, 1983b.

Garrison, W. T., Earls, F. J., and Kindlon, D. "An Application of the Pictorial Scale of Perceived Competence and Social Acceptance in an Epidemiological Survey." *Journal of Abnormal Child Psychology*, 1983, *11*, 367-378.

Garrison, W. T., Earls, F. J., and Kindlon, D. "Temperament Characteristics in the Third Year of Life and Adjustment at School Entry." *Journal of Clinical Child Psychology*, 1984, *13*, 298-303.

Ghodsian, M., Zajicek, E., and Wolkind, S. "A Longitudinal Study of Maternal Depression and Child Behavior Problems." *Journal of Child Psychology and Psychiatry*, 1984, *25* (1), 91-109.

Ghodsian, M., Zajicek-Coleman, E., and Wolkind, S. "Comparative Study of Social and Family Correlates of Children's Behaviour Ratings." Unpublished manuscript, 1982.

Goldberg, S. "Premature Birth: Consequences for the Parent-Infant Relationship." *American Scientist*, 1979, *67*, 214-220.

Harter, S. "The Perceived Competence Scale for Children." *Child Development*, 1982, *53*, 87-97.

Kaplan, D. N., and Mason, E. A. "Maternal Reactions to Premature Birth Viewed as an Acute Emotional Disorder." *American Journal of Orthopsychiatry*, 1960, *30*, 539-552.

Kendall, R. E., Wainwright, S., Hailey, A., and Shannon, B. "Postpartum Depression." *Psychological Medicine*, 1976, *6*, 297-302.

Leifer, A., Leiderman, P., Barnett, C., and Williams, J. "Effects of Mother-Infant Separation on Maternal Attachment Behavior." *Child Development*, 1972, *43*, 1203-1218.

Lewis, M., Feiring, C., McGuffog, C., and Jaskir, J. "Predicting Psychopathology in Six-Year-Olds from Early School Relations." *Child Development*, 1984, *55*, 123-136.

Lewis, M., and Schaeffer, S. "Peer Behavior and Mother-Infant Behavior in Maltreated Children." In M. Lewis and L. Rosenblum (eds.), *The Uncommon Child*. New York: Plenum, 1981.

Lewis, M., and Starr, M. D. "Developmental Community." In J. Osofsky (ed.), *Handbook of Infant Development*. New York: Wiley, 1979.

Links, P. S. "Community Surveys of the Prevalence of Childhood Psychiatric Disorders: A Review." *Child Development*, 1983, *54*, 531-548.

Moss, P., and Lewis, I. "Mental Distress in Mothers of Preschool Children in Inner London." *Psychological Medicine*, 1977, *7*, 641-652.

Orr, S. T., and James, S. "Maternal Depression in an Urban Pediatric Practice: Implications for Health Care Delivery." *American Journal of Public Health*, 1984, *74*, 363-365.

Plomin, R. "Childhood Temperament." In B. Lahey and A. Kazdin (eds.), *Advances in Clinical Child Psychology*. Vol. 6. New York: Plenum, 1982.

Richman, N. "Short-Term Outcome of Behavior Problems in Three-Year-Old Children." In P. J. Graham (ed.), *Epidemiological Approaches in Child Psychiatry*. London: Academic Press, 1977.

Richman, N. "Depression in Mothers of Young Children." *Journal of the Royal Society of Medicine*, 1978, *71*, 489-493.

Richman, N., Stevenson, J., and Graham, P. "Prevalence of Behavior Problems in Three-Year-Old Children: An Epidemiological Study in a London Borough." *Journal of Child Psychology and Psychiatry*, 1975, *16*, 277-287.

Richman, N., Stevenson, J., and Graham, P. *Preschool to School: A Behavioral Study*. New York: Academic Press, 1982.

Seashore, M., Leifer, A., Barnett, C., and Leiderman, P. "The Effects of Denial of Early Mother-Infant Interaction on Maternal Self-Confidence." *Journal of Personality and Social Psychology*, 1973, *26*, 369-378.

Spitzer, R., Endicott, J., and Robins, E. *Research Diagnostic Criteria for a Selected Group of Functional Disorders*. (3rd ed.) New York: Biometrics Research, New York State Psychiatric Institute, 1977.

Thomas, A., and Chess, S. *Temperament and Development*. New York: Brunner/Mazel, 1977.

Thomas, A., and Chess, S. *The Dynamics of Psychological Development*. New York: Brunner/Mazel, 1980.

Thomas, A., and Chess, S. "Genesis and Evolution of Behavioral Disorders: From Infancy to Early Adult Life." *American Journal of Psychiatry*, 1984, *141* (1), 1-9.

Weintraub, M., and Wolf, B. M. "Effects of Stress and Social Supports on Mother-Child Interactions in Single- and Two-Parent Families." *Child Development*, 1983, *54*, 1297-1311.

Weissman, M., Prusoff, B., Gammon, G. D., Merikangas, K. R., Leckman, J., and Kidd, K. "Psychopathology in the Children of Depressed and Normal Parents." *Journal of the American Academy of Child Psychiatry*, 1984, *23* (1), 78-84.

Welner, Z., Welner, A., McCrary, M. D., and Leonard, M. A. "Psychopathology in Children of Inpatients with Depression: A Controlled Study." *Journal of Nervous and Mental Disorders*, 1977, *164*, 408-413.

Werner, E. E., and Smith, R. S. *Vulnerable but Invincible: A Longitudinal Study of Resilient Children and Youth.* New York: McGraw-Hill, 1981.

Wolkind, S., Zajicek, E., and Ghodsian, M. "Continuities in Maternal Depression." *International Journal of Family Psychiatry*, 1980, *1*, 167-182.

Yalom, I., Lunde, D., Moos, R., and others. "Postpartum Blues Syndrome: A Description and Related Variables." *Archives of General Psychiatry*, 1968, *18*, 16-27.

William T. Garrison is director of pediatric psychology at the Baystate Medical Center in Springfield, Massachusetts, and assistant professor of pediatrics at the University of Massachusetts Medical School. His research interests include the epidemiology and treatment of behavioral disorders in young children.

Felton J. Earls is director of the William Greenleaf Eliot Division of Child Psychiatry and professor of psychiatry (child) at the Washington University Schoool of Medicine in St. Louis, Missouri. His research activities span a broad range of topics including the social etiology of early child psychopathology, the offspring of psychiatrically ill parents, and adolescent health care.

Although some depressed mothers are withdrawn, others are highly engaged and intrusive. There are correspondences between the behavior of depressed mothers and their infants.

Face-to-Face Interactions of Depressed Mothers and Their Infants

Jeffrey F. Cohn, Reinaldo Matias, Edward Z. Tronick, David Connell, Karlen Lyons-Ruth

Infants and young children of depressed mothers are at increased risk for developmental problems. These problems range from disturbances in the regulation of affect (Gaensbauer and others, 1984; Zahn-Waxler and others, 1984a, 1984b), the inability to achieve secure attachment (Gaensbauer and others, 1984; Radke-Yarrow and others, 1985), and other socioemotional behaviors (Sameroff and others, 1982; Zahn-Waxler and others, 1984a, 1984b) to poorer performance on measures of intellectual ability (Cohler and others, 1977; Gamer and others, 1977; Sameroff and others, 1982) and

---

This study was supported in part by Biomedical Research Support Grant Program (BRSG) Grant RR07084-18 awarded to Jeffrey F. Cohn and National Institute of Mental Health (NIMH) Grant 35122 awarded to Karlen Lyons-Ruth. Portions of these data were presented as a part of a symposium entitled "Family Characteristics and Child Behavior as Precursors of Psychological Disorder: Longitudinal Perspectives on Children at Risk," at the biennial meeting of the Society for Research in Child Development, Toronto, April, 1985.

in academic achievement (Baldwin and others, 1982). Furthermore, there is increasing evidence that affective disorders aggregate in families (Cytryn and others, 1984), which suggests that children of depressed parents are at increased risk for affective disorders as well.

What are the sources of this increased liability? What are the mechanisms through which parental pathology influences the child? Unquestionably, in some proportion of families, especially in the case of bipolar illness, a genetic component is likely (Nurnberger and Gershon, 1984). However, the range and extent of suboptimal outcomes associated with having a depressed parent cannot be attributed simply to genetic factors either in isolation or in conjunction with particular rearing environments (Cytryn and others, 1984; Beardslee and others, 1983). Thus, it is important to understand how parental depression is experienced by infants and young children and how that experience might contribute to their increased chances of impaired socioemotional and intellectual development.

Developmental studies of depressed mothers and infants have tended to emphasize the depressed mother's emotional unavailability and withdrawal (Sameroff and others, 1982). This emphasis is informed in part by the extensive findings that relate maternal warmth and contingent responsiveness in normal populations to positive child outcomes (Bates and others, 1985; Clarke-Stewart, 1973; Matas, Arend, and Sroufe, 1978). Although emotional unavailability, hopelessness, and withdrawal are likely to be associated with maternal depression, confusion, irritability, and, in the case of bipolar depression, grandiosity and euphoria are equally likely (Radke-Yarrow and others, 1985; Weissman and Paykel, 1974). For obvious reasons, the latter types of emotional expression have not commanded much attention in studies of not-at-risk infants or children, and hence only recently have coding or rating systems been designed to describe them (Vaughn, Taraldson, Crichton, and Egeland, 1980). Previous work in this area has tended to ignore the range of potential individual differences among depressed mothers and the processes through which a mother's depression may influence her infant's development.

Our Hypotheses

A major emphasis of our work is the communication of affect between mothers and their infants and its relation to infant socioemotional and cognitive development. Face-to-face interactions, in our view, are a primary way in which behavior and personality disorder may be transmitted from parent to infant. During interaction with primary caregivers, the infant responds to the affective characteristics of the caregiver's behavior in a way that is specific to that affect (Tronick, 1981). Over time, the infant's emotional reactions are internalized and guide his or her future evaluations of new situations (Cohn and Tronick, 1982; Tronick, Cohn, and Shea, 1986). According to this hypothesis, the infant whose predominant experience during interactions is one of distress will be less positive and more negative, or at least more wary, in his or her response to new situations.

Social interaction is also a context for the acquisition of skilled behavior (Bruner, 1974). One of the young infant's earliest tasks, following the achievement of state regulation, is to acquire the requisite skills needed to regulate social exchange (Sander, 1962). Initially, exchanges are focused entirely on themselves (Tronick, 1981), and each partner's goal can be defined as the achievement of shared positive engagement. With development, objects become increasingly important to the infant, and he or she must then acquire the skills to share reference to objects (Tronick, 1981). According to data from Bruner (Ratner and Bruner, 1978) and from studies of social referencing (Campos and Stenberg, 1981), the ability to share external referents emerges during the second half-year. Social interaction, then, provides experiences essential both to the infant's motivation and to his or her acquisition of prelinguistic and sensorimotor skills, such as turn-taking and shared referencing that contribute to subsequent development.

Simulated Depression in Face-to-Face Interactions

To examine these hypotheses, we have completed a series of studies of normal infants and of infants at risk because of maternal depression. To test the hypotheses that infants are sensitive to the affective message of their mother's behavior, we asked mothers to simulate the sad, withdrawn aspects of depression during face-to-face interactions (Cohn and Tronick, 1982, 1983). We hypothesized that if infants were responsive to their mother's affective expression, they would respond in a manner that was specific to depressed affect. Moreover, if interaction is indeed a skilled activity (Bruner, 1974), then we expected to see that the infants would make goal-directed attempts to effect a change in their mother's behavior. And, third, if the emotions generated during interactions carry over into new situations, we expected that infant reactions to simulated depression would continue to influence behavior even after mothers again behaved normally.

Briefly, these predictions were confirmed. When mothers interacted with sad affect, their infants responded in a way totally unlike their behavior in unperturbed interactions. Infants showed a pattern of brief smiling and then, when the mother continued to act depressed, turning away. Generally, infants showed a pattern in which they alternated between crying or fussing and turning away or looking at the mother with a wary expression. Especially important, this pattern of distressed behavior carried over into periods in which the mother behaved normally. These findings, which have been replicated by Field (1984), support the hypotheses that the infant's face-to-face behavior is closely related to the mother's and that patterns of emotional adaptation will influence behavior in other contexts.

The Clinical Study

In our recent work, we have used these hypotheses to guide our study of depressed mothers and their infants. We wanted to learn whether the simulated-depression results would generalize to a clinical population and whether there would be developmental sequelae to an infant's experience with a depressed mother. Specifically, we asked whether (1) depressed mothers would behave in a disengaged way similar to what we had modeled in the simulated-depression study; (2) infants of depressed mothers would be disengaged and lack contingent responsiveness during interactions with their mothers; (3) the negative emotions characteristic of structured interactions would persist at other times. In the remainder of this chapter, we present what we have learned about the social interactions of depressed mothers and their infants, contrast this with what is known about the interactions of not-at-risk mother-infant pairs, and discuss directions for future research.

Methodology. We studied a subgroup of thirteen depressed mothers and their infants who were participating in the Family Support Project, an NIMH-funded intervention based in Cambridge, Massachusetts (Chapter Five in this volume). The babies were eight boys and five girls. All but two were born between thirty-seven and forty weeks gestational age. The two premature infants were born at thirty-six weeks.

Maternal depression was assessed at the time of family intake and again nine to eighteen months later with the Center for Epidemiological Studies Depression Scale (CES-D) (Radloff, 1977). The CES-D is widely used in epidemiologic studies and has been validated against standardized psychiatric interviews that use Research Diagnostic Criteria (Spitzer, Endicott, and Robins, 1978). The instrument's false-positive rate for depression is a low 6 percent (Myers and Weissman, 1980). The mean CES-D score for our sample was well within the range for outpatient depressives, and these scores were stable over the following nine to eighteen months.

The mothers had high levels of chronic depression, but they also had high rates of other factors identified by epidemiologic studies as risk factors for childhood behavior disorder and the development of psychopathology (Robins, 1974; Rutter and others, 1974). These included reported child abuse or neglect ($n = 4$), previous psychiatric hospitalization ($n = 3$), absence of the father from the home ($n = 7$), and low socioeconomic status (SES) (all).

When the babies were between six and seven months old, project staff who were known to the families went to their homes and videotaped the mothers and infants. A six-minute structured face-to-face interaction followed a forty-minute period of naturalistic observation. For the naturalistic observation, the mothers were told that we wanted to observe a typical segment of their infant's day and were asked to behave as they normally would. For the structured interaction, the infant was in an infant seat placed on a table and the mother sat in a facing chair. A mirror placed at an angle to the mother permitted us to record frontal views of both the mother and her baby with a single camera. This produced tapes similar to those obtained in our laboratory studies, which used two cameras yoked to a split-screen generator. The six-minute structured interaction consisted of two three-minute play periods. During the first, no toys were permitted; during the second, the mother was given a toy to include in the play. This chapter includes data from the three-minute play period without toys.

Mother and infant behavior during the structured face-to-face interaction was encoded using behavioral descriptors and a one-second sampling interval (modifying the technique of Tronick, Als, and Brazelton, 1980). Mother and infant behavior during the period of naturalistic observation was described subsequently by means of separate rating scales for each partner. Different research assistants scored the spontaneous and the structured interactions. By observing both kinds of interactions and describing them with related techniques, we were able to assess whether patterns of behavior were stable across situations.

For the structured interaction, mother's and baby's facial and vocal expression, direction of gaze, and quality of touching were scored separately from the videotape. These data were then combined to create hierarchical behavioral descriptors. For the mother, the principal descriptors were Anger/Poke, Disengage, Elicit, and Play. *Anger/Poke* refers to instances in which the mother is either speaking to or handling her infant in a grossly angry way or is roughly poking or pulling at her infant. *Disengage* refers to instances in which the mother is neutral in affective expression and not interacting with her infant; it includes diverse ways in which the mother may be uninvolved. She may be leaning back and away from her infant, looking away, or passively watching her baby. *Elicit* refers to actions that are rapid or staccato in nature and appear intended to get baby's attention. This includes snapping fingers or bringing her head quickly into the infant's line of vision. *Play* includes all instances of positive affective expression—for example, smiles and singsong vocalizations. These codes permitted us to quantify both normal maternal behavior and the range of individual differences that have been described anecdotally in the clinical literature (Weissman and Paykel, 1974): disengaged, sad, or unexpressive, and agitated, angry, or overstimulating.

Related codes were used to describe the infant's facial and vocal expression and direction of gaze during the structured interactions. *Protest* refers to negative affective expressions of fussing, grimacing, or crying.

Look Away, Object, and Attend all refer to neutral to slightly negative affective expression with gaze directed either away from the mother and not toward an object, away from the mother but toward an object, or toward the mother's face. Objects during this three-minute interaction segment were those naturally present, such as the infant seat shoulder strap or a body part used as an object (for example, mother's "butterfly" hands). *Play* refers to positive facial expressions and gaze directed at the mother.

For the description of mother's and infant's behavior during the period of naturalistic observation, we used rating scales that paralleled the behavioral coding of play interactions. These included mother ratings of Number of Verbalizations, Flatness of Affect, Anger, Covertly Hostile and Interfering contact, and infant ratings of Activity Level, Affect, Social Responsiveness, and Reciprocal Play. The mother ratings are described in more detail in Lyons-Ruth, Connell, Zoll, and Stahl (in press).

Findings. During the face-to-face interactions, the mothers were extremely variable in two overlapping dimensions: positivity or level of engagement and intrusiveness or expressions of anger.

At the extreme of disengagement, a small number of mothers, (M-Disengaged, Figure 1) showed a pattern similar to clinical descriptions (Weissman and Paykel, 1974; Field, 1984) of depressed mothers and to what we modeled in our simulated-depression study. These mothers were each disengaged for 75 percent or more of the interaction time. They slouched back in their chairs, turned away from the infant, or spoke to the baby in an expressionless voice with little facial expression. They were seldom positive and looked very much like the mothers in our depression-analogue study.

A second group of mothers (M-Mixed) showed similarly low proportions of positive expression but high rates of eliciting behavior. These mothers appeared to want to engage their babies, and they used many of the eliciting behaviors seen in studies of not-at-risk mother-infant pairs, but they didn't seem able to expand their affective range. They were unable to play. Only the third group (M-Positive) was able to do so: These mothers showed a broad range of neutral to positive affective expression and were positive in their affective expression at least 35 percent of the time.

The M-Disengaged, M-Mixed, and M-Positive groups of mothers represent an extreme variability of positive expression from disengaged and flat to highly engaged and positive; the remaining six mothers all showed high levels of engagement, but their engagement was primarily intrusive and negative. These mothers (M-Intrusive) had low proportions of positive expression and high proportions of expressed anger or of poking or pulling at their infant (minimum proportion was 25 percent).

With the exception of M-Positive, these patterns are strikingly unlike those in studies of normal mothers conducted by ourselves and others (Kaye and Fogel, 1980; Fafonti-Milenković and Užgiris, 1979). Our own

Figure 1. Individual Differences Among Depressed Mothers in the Percent of Time Spent in Behavioral States During Face-to-Face Interactions with Their Infants

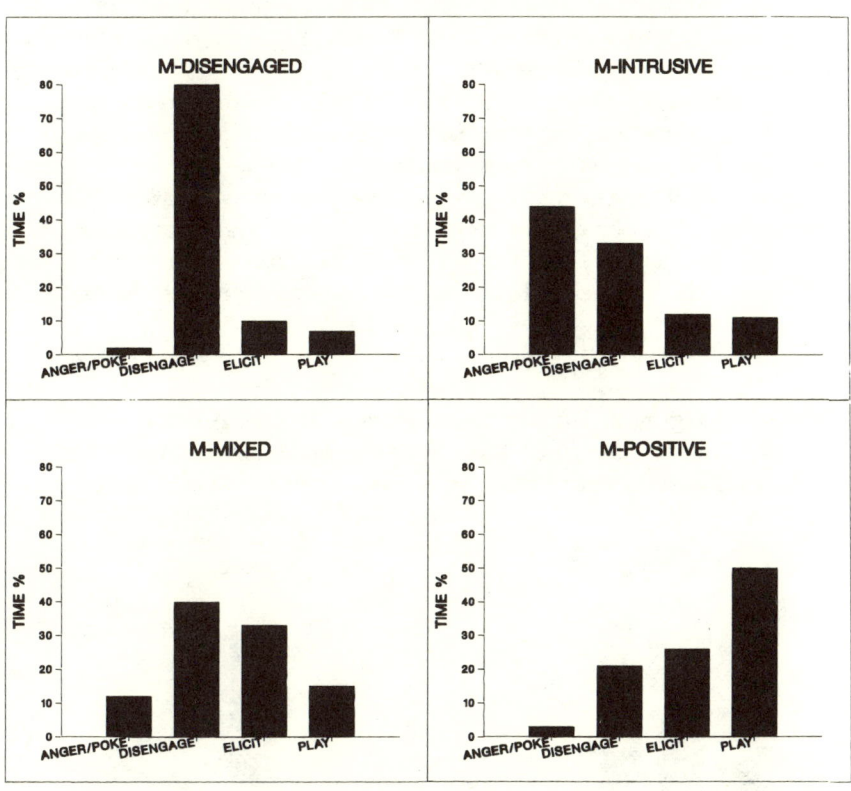

work, conducted in Amherst, Massachusetts, draws women from middle- to working-class urban and suburban communities; we have found that mothers of six-month-old babies are in Play (positive affective expression) an average of 42 percent of the time (and this increases by the time the babies are nine months old). Kaye and Fogel (1980), in their study of urban working-class women, reported the proportion of positive affective expression to be only slightly less, approximately 35 percent at six months. In the Cambridge depressed sample, only four mothers had proportions of Play in the range of 30 to 45 percent, and one of these had an equally high porportion of Anger/Poke. Only one mother had a proportion of Play that exceeded the Amherst mean. Moreover, neither the Kaye and Fogel nor the Tronick and others study reported any trace of angry expressions or other intrusive behavior. Indeed, the only previous studies that have noted intrusive or overstimulating (but not angry) maternal behavior have been studies of premature infants and their mothers (Bakeman and Brown, 1980; Field, 1977). The angry and intrusive behavior that characterized almost one-half of the mothers here is extremely atypical.

The infants' behavior was far less variable than the mothers'. The infants were highly withdrawn and seldom showed positive affective expression. Whereas Amherst infants at six months are in Play an average of 15 percent of the time, only one infant here was in Play for an equal percentage of time, and none was in Play for a greater percentage. Another important difference with the Amherst data is the percentage of infants' time in Object. During interactions with their mothers, infants of this age typically attend to objects two to three times more than that found here.

Figure 2 shows the infants' profiles that correspond to each of the four groups of mothers. There are some important correspondences

Figure 2. Individual Differences Among Infants in the Percent of Time Spent in Behavioral States During Face-to-Face Interactions with Their Depressed Mothers

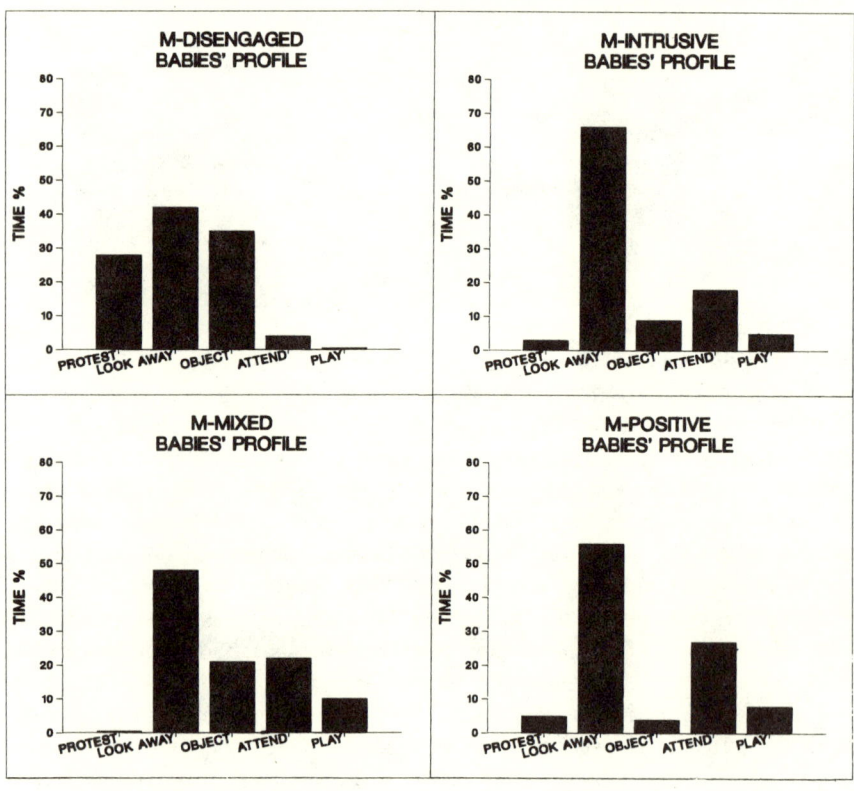

between infant's behavior and mother's classification. Two infant behaviors—Look Away and Protest—closely correspond to maternal behavior and classification. Infants of the intrusive mothers spent almost 70 percent of their time looking away. They also had one of the lowest proportions in Object. The strongest relation, however, is that between the mother-classification M-Disengaged and infant Protest. The most disturbing behavior for these infants was the pattern of maternal disengagement. Not even high rates of poking provoked comparable upset.

Although there was a significant correlation between the proportions of mother Play and infant Play ($r = .51$), the low proportions of infant Play suggest little actual dependence in Play between mothers and infants. Moreover, with the exception of the M-Positive group, there was no indication of mother or infant matching the other's play. For instance, among the Intrusive mothers, the odds were better than two to one that the mother would be in a state other than Play when her baby was in Play. The M-Intrusive mothers would continue to poke or pull at their infant rather than to match the infant's affective state. This is extremely different from what we have found in not-at-risk samples. Typically, less than 5 percent of the time are mothers not in Play when their infant is. More generally, a most dramatic difference between these and normal interactions was the mothers' failure to provide a positive affective frame within which their babies could cycle to and from a positive state (Cohn and Tronick, in press).

This failure to provide a positive frame for their babies was part of a more general lack of contingent responsiveness that is evident in the videotapes. With few exceptions, there was little indication of turn-taking or mutual responsiveness. These observations were supported quantitatively by contingency analyses. Using time-series regression (Gottman, 1981; McCleary and Hay, 1980), we examined whether the mothers or infants were showing any evidence of contingent responsiveness to the other. The behavior of only four mothers and two infants was contingent upon the partner's previous or concurrent behavior. This contrasts with what we have found in not-at-risk mother-infant pairs of similar ages. In normal dyads, evidence of contingent responsiveness to the partner is found in over half the mothers and one-third or more of the infants.

Maternal affective expression during the spontaneous interactions was consistent with that observed during the structured face-to-face interactions. Both the maternal profiles and the quantitative scores on which they were based correlated with ratings of comparable behavior during the spontaneous interactions. Mothers whose affect was most withdrawn during the spontaneous interactions tended to be the same mothers whose affect was most withdrawn during the face-to-face interactions. Flatness of Affect during spontaneous interactions correlated -.50 with Play; Warmth correlated .45 with Play. Ratings of Anger correlated .64 with Anger/Poke.

The continuity across situations suggests that there may be individual differences related to the expression of positivity and anger.

Depressed mothers, however, especially those who seem most irritable and negative, may have ways of coping with their own emotions in such a way as to protect their babies. The period of spontaneous interactions, because it did not compel the mothers to interact, allowed us to compare typical behavior with that seen in the more stressful situation in which the mothers are asked to interact. We found that, when free to interact with their babies or not, the more intrusive mothers tended to avoid them. They initiated fewer interactions and were more likely to spend less total time with their babies. Mothers high in Anger/Poke spent less time in the same room with their babies and, when present, were less likely to talk to them. The only time that they were more likely interact was in comforting or caretaking situations.

We also found some continuity between the infants' behavior during the two situations. Babies who were more positive during the face-to-face interaction were more often positive and less often negative during the period of spontaneous interaction. In either situation, however, the actual proportion of time in which babies were positive in expression tended to be little.

These interactions were strikingly unlike those in normal samples. The mothers behaved in a relatively detached manner or with great impatience and insensitivity toward their infants. Infants' behavior had high proportions of looking away and, in the case of the Disengaged mothers, fussing and crying. Maternal positive affective expression, when it did occur, caused little increase in infant positive affective expression. Although there was a tendency for the mothers and infants to match the proportion of positive and negative affective expression, the latter was far more pronounced. What matching did occur, however, was not the result of any turn-taking or contingency between mother's and infant's behavior, as is the case in the interactions of normal dyads. We found few instances of contingency between the mother's or infant's behavior and the concurrent or preceding behavior of the other. There was little that could be considered skilled performance in the regulation of these interactions.

Implications. What are the implications of these findings? First, we must recognize that there is far more variability in the behavior of depressed mothers than previously has been appreciated. Depressed mothers are not uniformly withdrawn and restricted in their range of emotional expression. There appear to be two principal ways in which depression that is most often thought of in connection with affective disorders and parenting does exist and has a powerful impact on the baby. These data suggest that many women, however, become highly intrusive and are likely to express anger toward their baby. This kind of behavior has not been systematically studied.

Do the types of behavior found here constitute stable individual differences in the expression of maternal depression? In the present case, we found stability between two situations, but replication over longer time periods is essential. Also, we need to pay far greater attention to ways in which mothers may adapt or cope with their own emotional expression to shield their babies. Intrusive mothers appeared aversive, but primarily in a situation in which they felt compelled to play. When free to regulate their level of involvement, they tended to remain distant, even remaining in separate rooms from their baby. They would respond to their baby's needs for comforting, and when they did so they seemed more able to behave in an appropriate and caring way. Theoretically, this suggests that the effects of maternal depression may be mediated either through distortions of face-to-face interaction or through a diminution of such experience. Depressed mothers, especially those who feel hostile, may cope by limiting the kinds of contact they have and, in particular, by limiting play interactions. Within limits, this may be adaptive for both mother and baby.

The Need for Further Research

There is increasing indication that infants of depressed mothers are at risk for a wide range of developmental problems as early as the first year of life. We have reported elsewhere (Chapter Five in this volume; Cohn and others, 1985) that Bayley scores of infants of depressed mothers lag behind those of matched controls at twelve months, even when the mother's intellectual level is covaried. Others (Sameroff and others, 1982) have reported Bayley differences related to maternal depression by eighteen months. Our view is that one source of these delays is the infant's experience during social interactions. The infant of a depressed mother experiences more negative interactions with fewer opportunities to learn to coordinate action formats involving shared meaning and reference to external objects. Negative emotions developed in interaction contexts carry over into other situations as well.

Alternatively, as we have suggested, it is possible that there is simply less opportunity for interactions to occur. The mother may be intentionally limiting her contact to caretaking situations. We do not know whether the consequences of distorted interaction are the same as those of infrequent and largely caretaking-mediated interactions. To begin answering such questions, we must make systematic assessments of the infant's day and begin to develop more focused outcome measures than those that have been used in the past (for example, than the Bayley). We need instruments that are sensitive to the infant's predominant mood, sense of effectance, and competence in social and nonsocial exchanges (Yarrow and others, 1983). And, closer conceptual ties are needed between our process and outcome measures.

We also need to delimit maternal depression more carefully. As noted above, maternal depression was one of several risk factors characteristic of the families we studied. In practice, depression is likely to covary with other sources of liability. It is important to use screening techniques that have high sensitivity to depression and then to follow these up with structured psychiatric interviews using Research Diagnostic Criteria and carefully controlling for other risk factors. Only in this way can we disentangle the multiple sources of risk and discern what is specific about maternal depression. There are strong theoretic reasons for the hypothesis that maternal depression is a significant risk factor, but better controlled studies are essential to validate this hypothesis. Particular care is needed in separating the potentially differential effects of acute and nonreoccurring depression (such as postpartum depression), chronic and episodic depression, and the relatively stable depressive symptoms that may be associated with personality disorders.

References

Bakeman, R., and Brown, J. V. "Early Interaction: Consequences for Social and Mental Development." *Child Development*, 1980, *51*, 437–447.

Baldwin, A. L., Cole, R. E., and Baldwin, C. P. "Parental Pathology, Family Interaction, and the Competence of the Child in School." *Monographs of the Society for Research in Child Development*, Serial No. 197, 1982, *47* (5), entire issue.

Bates, J. E., Maslin, C. A., and Frankel, K. A. "Attachment Security, Mother-Child Interaction, and Temperament as Predictors of Behavior-Problem Ratings at Age Three Years." In I. Bretherton and E. Waters (eds.), *Growing Points of Attachment Theory and Research. Monographs of the Society for Research in Child Development*, Serial No. 209, 1985, *50* (1-2), 167–193.

Beardslee, W. R., Bemporad, J., Keller, M. B., and Klerman, G. L. "Children of Parents with Major Affective Disorder: A Review." *American Journal of Psychiatry*, 1983, *54*, 1254–1268.

Bruner, J. S. "The Organization of Early Skilled Action." In M.P.M. Richards (ed.), *The Interaction of a Child into a Social World*. Cambridge, England: Cambridge University Press, 1974.

Campos, J. J., and Stenberg, C. "Perception, Appraisal, and Emotion: The Onset of Social Referencing." In M. E. Lamb and L. R. Sherrod (eds.), *Infant Social Cognition: Empirical and Theoretical Considerations*. Hillsdale, N.J.: Erlbaum, 1981.

Clarke-Stewart, K. A. "Interactions Between Mothers and Their Young Children: Characteristics and Consequences." *Monographs of the Society for Research in Child Development*, Serial No. 153, 1973, *38*, (6–7), entire issue.

Cohler, B. J., Grunebaum, H. U., Weiss, J. L., Gamer, E., and Gallant, D. H. "Disturbance of Attention Among Schizophrenic, Depressed, and Well Mothers and Their Children." *Journal of Child Psychology and Psychiatry*, 1977, *18*, 115–135.

Cohn, J. F., Matias, R., Connell, D., and Lyons-Ruth, K. "Face-to-Face Interaction and Developmental Differences." In S. Campbell (chair), *Family and Child Characteristics as Predictors of Psychological Disorder: Longitudinal Perspectives on Children at Risk*. Paper presented at the biennial meeting of the Society for Research in Child Development, Toronto, April 1985.

Cohn, J. F., and Tronick, E. Z. "Communicative Rules and the Sequential Structure of Infant Behavior During Normal and Depressed Interaction." In E. Z. Tronick (ed.), *Social Interchange in Infancy: Affect, Cognition, and Communication.* Baltimore, Md.: University Park Press, 1982.

Cohn, J. F., and Tronick, E. Z. "Three-Month-Old Infants' Reaction to Simulated Maternal Depression." *Child Development,* 1983, *54,* 185-193.

Cohn, J. F., and Tronick, E. Z. "Continuity and Change from Three to Nine Months in the Sequence of Mother-Infant Dyadic States During Face-to-Face Interaction." *Developmental Psychology,* in press, *23.*

Cytryn, L., McKnew, D. H., Zahn-Waxler, C., Radke-Yarrow, M., Gaensbauer, T. J., Harmon, R. J., and Lamour, M. "A Developmental View of Affective Disturbances in the Children of Affectively Ill Parents." *American Journal of Psychiatry,* 1984, *141,* 219-222.

Fafouti-Milenković M., and Užgiris, I. Č. "The Mother-Infant Communication System." In I. Č. Užgiris (ed.), *Social Interaction and Communication During Infancy.* no. 4. San Francisco: Jossey-Bass, 1979.

Field, T. M. "Effects of Early Separation, Interactive Deficits, and Experimental Manipulations on Infant-Mother Face-to-Face Interactions." *Child Development,* 1977, *48,* 763-771.

Field, T. M. "Early Interactions Between Infants and Their Postpartum Depressed Mothers." *Infant Behavior and Development,* 1984, *7,* 517-522.

Gaensbauer, T. J., Harmon, R. J., Cytryn, L., and McKnew, D. H. "Social and Affective Development in Infants with a Manic-Depressive Parent." *American Journal of Psychiatry,* 1984, *141,* 223-229.

Gamer, E., Gallant, D., Grunebaum, H. U., and Cohler, B. J. "Children of Psychotic Mothers: Performance of Three-Year-Old Children on Tests of Attention." *Archives of General Psychiatry,* 1977, *34,* 592-597.

Gottman, J. M. *Time-Series Analysis: A Comprehensive Introduction for Social Scientists.* New York: Academic Press, 1981.

Kaye, K., and Fogel, A. "The Temporal Structure of Face-to-Face Communication Between Mothers and Infants." *Developmental Psychology,* 1980, *16,* 454-464.

Lyons-Ruth, K., Connell, D., Zoll, D., and Stahl, J. "Infants Maltreatment, Maternal Behavior, and Infant Attachment Behavior." *Developmental Psychology,* in press.

McCleary, R., and Hay, R. A. *Applied Time-Series Analysis for the Social Sciences.* Beverly Hills, Calif.: Sage, 1980.

Matas, L., Arend, R. A., and Sroufe, L. A. "Continuity of Adaptation in the Second Year: The Relationship Between Quality of Attachment and Later Competence." *Child Development,* 1978, *49,* 547-556.

Myers, J. K., and Weissman, M. M. "Use of a Self-Report Symptom Scale to Detect Depression in a Community Sample." *American Journal of Psychiatry,* 1980, *137,* 1081-1084.

Nurnberger, J., and Gershon, E. S. "Genetics of Affective Disorders." In R. Post and P. Ballenger (eds.), *Neurobiology of Mood Disorders.* Baltimore, Md.: Williams and Wilkins, 1984.

Radke-Yarrow, M., Cummings, E. M., Kuczynski, L., and Chapman, M. "Patterns of Attachment in Two- and Three-Year-Olds in Normal Families and Families with Parental Depression." *Child Development,* 1985, *56,* 884-893.

Radloff, L. S. "The CES-D Scale: A Self-Report Depression Scale for Research in the General Population." *Applied Psychological Measurement,* 1977, *3,* 385-401.

Ratner, N. K., and Bruner, J. S. "Games, Social Exchange, and the Acquisition of Language." *Journal of Child Language,* 1978, *5,* 391-401.

Robins, L. *Deviant Children Grown Up.* New York: Krieger, 1974.
Rutter, M., Yule, B., Quinton, D., Rowlands, O., Yule, W., and Berger, M. "Attainment and Adjustment in Two Geographical Areas: III: Some Factors Accounting for Area Differences." *British Journal of Psychiatry,* 1974, *123,* 520-533.
Sameroff, A., Seifer, R., and Zax, M. "Early Development of Children at Risk for Emotional Disorder." *Monographs of the Society for Research in Child Development,* Serial No. 199, 1982, *47* (7), entire issue.
Sander, L. "Issue in Early Mother-Child Interaction." *Journal of the American Academy of Child Psychiatry,* 1962, *1,* 141-166.
Spitzer, R. L., and Endicott, J., and Robins, E. "Research Diagnostic Criteria: Rationale and Reliability." *Archives of General Psychiatry,* 1978, *36,* 773-782.
Tronick, E. Z. "Infant Communicative Intent: The Infant's Reference to Social Interaction." In R. Stark (ed.), *Language Behavior in Infancy.* New York: Elsevier, 1981.
Tronick, E. Z., Als, H., and Brazelton, T. B. "Monadic Phases: A Structural Descriptive Analysis of Infant-Mother Face-to-Face Interaction." *Merrill-Palmer Quarterly of Behavior and Development,* 1980, *26,* 3-24.
Tronick, E. Z., Cohn, J. F., and Shea, E. "The Transfer of Affect Between Mother and Infant." In M. Yogman and T. B. Brazelton (eds.), *Affective Development in Infancy.* Norwood, N.J.: Ablex, 1986.
Vaughn, B. E., Taraldson, B., Crichton, L., and Egeland, B. "Relationships Between Neonatal Behavioral Organization and Infant Behavior During the First Year of Life." *Infant Behavior and Development,* 1980, *3,* 47-66.
Weissman, M. M., and Paykel, E. S. *The Depressed Woman: A Study of Social Relationships.* Chicago: University of Chicago Press, 1974.
Yarrow, L. J., McQuiston, S., MacTurk, R. H., McCarthy, M. E., Klein, R. P., and Vietze, P. M. "Assessment of Mastery Motivation During the First Year of Life: Contemporaneous and Cross-Age Relationships." *Developmental Psychology,* 1983, *19,* 159-171.
Zahn-Waxler, C., Cummings, E. M., McKnew, D. H., and Radke-Yarrow, M. "Altruism, Aggression, and Social Interactions in Young Children with a Manic-Depressive Parent." *Child Development.* 1984a, *55,* 112-122.
Zahn-Waxler, C., Cummings, E. M., McKnew, D. H., and Radke-Yarrow, M. "Problem Behaviors and Peer Interactions of Young Children with a Manic-Depressive Parent." *American Journal of Psychiatry,* 1984b, *141,* 236-240.

Jeffrey F. Cohn is assistant professor of psychology in the Clinical Psychology Department at the University of Pittsburgh. His primary area of research is infant social development in normal and at-risk populations.

Reinaldo Matias is a graduate student in clinical psychology at the University of Pittsburgh.

Edward Z. Tronick is professor of psychology at the University of Massachusetts, Amherst. His research has focused on the social development of the young child in the United States and other countries.

David Connell is a lecturer in psychology in the Department of Psychiatry, Harvard Medical School, Cambridge Hospital, and a series analyst at Abt Associates, Cambridge, Massachusetts.

Karlen Lyons-Ruth is instructor in psychology in the Department of Psychiatry, Harvard Medical School, Cambridge Hospital. Her research interests have focused on the social and emotional development of normal and high-risk infants.

Recent studies suggest that maternal deprivation may predispose the infant to chronic depression, and the effects of early separations from the mother may provide a model for reactive depression.

Models for Reactive and Chronic Depression in Infancy

Tiffany Field

Infants appear to differ in their responsivity to social stimulation from birth because of different genetic backgrounds as well as prenatal and perinatal experiences. Mothers (or caregivers) learn to read their infants' affective displays (facial expressions, vocalizations, and gaze behavior) and modulate their stimulation to meet their infants' individual stimulation and arousal-modulation needs. When this occurs, the infant's affect appears to be positive, the interaction harmonious (both behaviorally and physiologically), and a normal attachment or relationship appears to develop, thereby fostering the infant's affective development.

If either member of the dyad is unresponsive or if their relationship is disrupted by separation, affective disturbances may occur. The infant, for example, may be unresponsive because of higher sensory thresholds or less-developed arousal-modulation and information-processing skills, and the mother may be unable to modulate her stimulation accordingly. Alter-

---

This research was supported by National Institute of Mental Health (NIMH) Research Scientist Development Award Number MH00331. I wish to thank the mothers and infants who participated in this study and my collaborators Martin Reite, David Sandberg, Robert Garcia, Nitza Vega-Lahr, Sheri Goldstein, and Lisa Guy.

natively, the mother may be the source of affective disturbance by being unresponsive—for example, if she is experiencing postpartum depression. Or both mother and infant may be unresponsive following a separation, such as for the birth of another child.

Of the interaction situations we have studied, affective disturbances appear to be most pronounced in those dyads featuring a depressed infant or a mother experiencing postpartum depression and in dyads experiencing an early separation. That is, infants appear to experience affective disturbances when (1) they are chronically exposed to inadequate stimulation (depressed mother) or (2) their interactions are disrupted by separations and accompanying changes in their relationship. The former experience we think may predispose the infant to chronic depression, and the separation situation may provide a model for reactive depression.

Reactive Depression and Early Separation Experiences

Spitz (1946) observed depression in young infants following separation from their mothers. More recently, this separation experience has been described as a biphasic process of protest followed by despair (Bowlby, 1969; Robertson and Robertson, 1971). These descriptions, however, are based on anecdotal case studies. More systematic separation studies have been conducted with young nonhuman primates by several investigators (Harlow and Harlow, 1965; Levine and Coe, 1985; Reite and others, 1981; Suomi and others, 1976). The primate studies as well as a study on prolonged separations of human infants (Field, 1985) confirm the biphasic response to separation, describing a period of agitation followed by a period of depression.

Infant pigtail and bonnet monkeys monitored via surgically implanted telemetry during mother-infant separations generally reveal behavioral agitation followed by depression during the separation period (Reite and others, 1981; Reite and Snyder, 1982). Shortly after the separation, infant monkeys exhibited an agitation reaction with increased motor activity and frequent distress vocalizations. Depressed behaviors typically emerged shortly thereafter and persisted for the period of separation: The infant monkeys moved more slowly than normal, and their play behavior was diminished. Sleep disturbances included decreases in rapid eye movement (REM) sleep as well as an increase in the number of arousals and time spent awake. The behavioral agitation reaction that occurred immediately after separation was accompanied by increases in both heart rate and body temperature followed by decreases to below baseline (Reite, Short, Kaufman, Stynes, and Pauley, 1978).

Human infants and toddlers also showed agitated behavior and physiology during a period of separation from their mothers, and these behaviors diminished following their reunion (Field, 1985). In this study, the infants' and toddlers' behavioral and physiological responses to separation were monitored before, during, and after their mothers' hospitalization for the birth of a sibling. During these three periods, play sessions were videotaped while activity level and heart rate were monitored. In addition, nighttime sleep was time-lapse videotaped, and the parents completed questionnaires on changes in their infant's or toddler's behaviors. Increases in fussiness, activity level, heart rate, night wakings, and nighttime crying characterized the hospital period as one of agitation (see Table 1). Following the mother's return, decreases were noted in positive affect, activity level, heart rate, and active sleep, suggestive of "reactive depression." Changes noted by the parents were a greater-than-chance occurrence of clinging and aggressive behaviors, changes in eating and toileting, and sleep disturbances and illnesses that persisted following the mother's return from the hospital.

The infants appeared agitated by the mother's separation, even though they visited her at the hospital and were cared for by their fathers. The depression following the mother's return from the hospital may have related to the depressed affect, decreased animation, and exhausted behavior noted in the mother during this period. This behavior in the mother together with the arrival of a new sibling seemed to alter the relationship previously experienced by the mother and infant. Examples of the infants' disturbance were provided by the parents' comments such as, the infant "remained close to the parent," "wanted to be rocked and held," "reverted

Table 1. Means for Play and Sleep Behaviors of Infants/Toddlers Prior to, During, and Following Their Mother's Hospitalization

Behaviors	Baseline	Separation	Reunion	p Level
Play Behaviors (Percent time sample unit)				
Smiling	9	2	3	.01
Animation	22	15	16	.05
Aggression	2	8	7	.05
Fussiness	15	22	21	.05
Activity level (actometer)	26	35	21	.05
Heart rate (BPM)	117	131	110	.05
Sleep Behaviors				
Total sleep time (minutes)	580	645	575	.05
Latency to sleep (minutes)	28	21	19	.05
Number of night wakings	1	5	4	.05
Crying (minutes)	8	15	14	.05

to baby talk, whining, and screaming for attention," "destroyed his [or her] playroom," and "threatened to run a truck across the baby's head." Increased fantasy play among the infants and toddlers, interpreted as an act of coping on their part, was characterized by a number of themes that involved aggression against the new sibling—for example, knocking the building blocks onto the new baby.

The biphasic increase followed by a decrease in activity level of the infants and toddlers parallels the sequence of agitation followed by depression reported for young primate separations (Reite and others, 1981). Elevated tonic heart rate following her return may have been mediated by the activity level changes, as in somatic coupling of activity and heart rate (Obrist, 1981). Elevated activity level and heart rate have been attributed to activation of the sympathetic adrenergic system (Breese, Smith, Mueller, Howard, Prange, Lipton, Young, McKinney, and Lewis, 1973). Increased night wakings and crying during the mother's hospitalization are also suggestive of this being an agitated phase for the infants. Longer periods of sleep during this separation period may be a manifestation of conservation-withdrawal noted to follow physical or emotional stress in young infants (Emde, Harmon, Metcalf, Koening, and Wagonfeld, 1971; Engel and Schmale, 1972).

The decrease in activity level, depressed heart rate, and shorter periods of active sleep together with depressed or flat affect following the mother's return may be manifestations of depression, a period we have alluded to as one of experienced helplessness on the part of the infant. The decrease in active sleep periods during what appears to be a depressed phase may be a homeostatic coping mechanism, not unlike the infants' and toddlers' more active coping with the stress by increased fantasy play. Depressed activity and heart rate are commonly reported in helpless and passive coping situations; for example, Obrist and others (1974) observed these phenomena during an avoidance task in which the human subjects had no control—a situation in which beta-adrenergic influences were minimal. Bradycardia, associated with situations of helplessness, has also been attributed to parasympathetic activation or vagal tone (McCabe and Schneiderman, 1985). The arrival of a new sibling, a less active, tired mother, changes in play interactions, and an altered parent-infant relationship may be viewed by the infants or toddlers as situations over which they have very little control.

The primate and human infants may become agitated during separation from the mother due to the loss of an important source of stimulation and arousal modulation. Young monkeys and infants are noted to turn to their mothers for stimulation as well as for comfort in the face of arousing or stressful situations (Ainsworth, 1967; Bowlby, 1969). Reite and his colleagues had speculated that bonnet infants would fare better under separation stress than pigtail infants because the bonnet infants are typically adopted by aunts in the social group, but the bonnet infants also showed agitation despite being adopted.

Similarly, it has been suggested that the human infant may tolerate temporary separation if the father is actively involved and if visits to the mother in the hospital are possible (Legg, Sherick, and Wadland, 1974). Yet the infants in the Field (1985) separation study had the advantage of both father involvement and mother visits; nonetheless, they were distressed during the hospitalization. Adoptive aunts, in the case of bonnet monkeys, and fathers, in the case of human infants, who are often stressed themselves by the mother's absence, may not be as effective as mothers in modulating arousal. Indeed, fathers are consistently noted to engage in more arousing games with their infants (Clarke-Stewart, 1978; Field, 1978; 1981; Lamb, 1975; Parke, 1979; Yogman, 1981). Although arousing games are typically viewed as a positive feature of father-infant interactions, heightened levels of arousal may stimulate the sympathetic adrenergic system and result in agitated behavior. This behavioral complex is typically associated with active coping—in this case, active coping to recall the mother.

The emergence of depression as the separation continues may relate to a number of factors. Depression is typically accompanied by increased parasympathetic activation or increases in vagal tone (McCabe and Schneiderman, 1985). This may be a homeostatic mechanism offsetting the sympathetic arousal or agitation in the absence of effective arousal modulation, or it may result from inadequate amounts of stimulation and limited beta-adrenergic activity. Just as the aunts and fathers may be less effective at modulating arousal, they may provide less-than-optimal amounts and types of stimulation by virtue of their less familiarity with the infant's stimulation needs. Still another possibility is that the hypothalamic-pituitary–adrenal-cortical system is activated during helpless or passive-coping situations (McCabe and Schneiderman, 1985). The monkey infant who fails to recall the mother may experience helplessness just as the human infant who is confronted with an altered relationship due to the arrival of the new sibling may experience helplessness.

Depression may persist following the return of the mother because the mother and/or infant have changed in some way, thus altering the previous relationship. The separations of young primate and human infants are often accompanied by behavior changes that persist even following reunions. These data suggest that separation may be a sufficient condition for behavioral disorganization but not a necessary condition. In studies by Reite and his colleagues (Reite, 1983), alterations of the mother-infant relationship (by placing a vest on the mother, with or without holes for sucking, or by the addition of the mother's new baby to the group) induced behavioral and physiological depression, thus highlighting the importance of changes in their relationship independent of separation. The status of the relationship upon reunion may be as important as the separation itself. Changes in the individuals or changes in their relationship may preclude their being in tune with each other upon reunion.

Data on pigtail infants suggest that, although heart rate and arrhythmia values tended to return to baseline following reunion with the mother, the altered cardiac activity persisted for some infants (Seiler, Cullen, Zimmerman, and Reite, 1979). In another study on bonnet monkey infants (Reite and Snyder, 1982), persistent decreases in heart rate and body temperature were noted following reunion with the mother, "possibly reflecting a disturbance in the mother-infant relationship secondary to the mothers having come into estrus during the period of separation" (p. 117). As the authors suggested, "the infant was in a sense reacting physiologically to the persistent disruption of the mother-infant attachment bond, even though the mother was physically present" (p. 117). The mother being in estrus or the mother returning with a new infant would conceivably alter the previous mother-infant relationship. In another study by Reite and his colleagues (Reite, 1983), the mother was noted to reject her infant upon reunion, as she very busily groomed other members of the social group in an attempt to reinstate herself in the dominance hierarchy. It was only after a few days of grooming activity that the mother redirected her attention to her infant. The infant's physiology remained depressed during that stressful reunion period, even in the presence of the mother.

Similarly, the infants in the Field (1985) separation study remained depressed following the return of their mothers. This depression was attributed to exhaustion in the mother and an altered relationship between the mother and child during their play together. Thus, infants may remain depressed following reunions with their mothers because of temporary disequilibrium in their relationships.

The effects of separation on primate and human infants appear to be similar, even though the context in which the separations of human infants was studied inevitably confounded separation with an altered mother-infant relationship resulting from the arrival of a new sibling. That combination, however, revealed that it is not necessarily separation itself that contributes to the infant's depression but rather a missing source of stimulation and arousal modulation for the infant both during the separation and following the reunion.

Effects of Maternal Depression on Infant Behavior

Less favorable affective development has been reported for children reared by depressed mothers as opposed to mothers with other diagnoses or normal mothers (Cytryn, McKnew, Bartko, Lamour, and Hamovitt, 1982; Sameroff and Seifer, 1983). In addition, relationships have been reported between early interaction disturbances and later childhood problems (Bakeman and Brown, 1980; Field, Dempsey, and Shuman, 1983). Despite these apparent relationships, there are very few studies in the literature on early interactions between depressed mothers and their infants.

An attempt has been made to simulate maternal depression by asking mothers to "look depressed" during interactions with their infants (Cohn and Tronick, 1983). Although it is not clear that their infants responded to their "looking depressed" in the same way that infants would respond to naturally depressed mothers, the interactions in which mothers were instructed to "look depressed" resulted in disorganized, distressed behavior on the part of the infant. During this manipulation, the infants more frequently looked wary, averted their gaze, protested, and attempted to elicit responses from the mother, just as when the infant interacting with a still-faced mother attempts to reinstate a normal interaction (Tronick, Als, Adamson, Wise, and Brazelton, 1977). In the Cohn and Tronick (1983) study, the infants' distressed behavior continued even after the mothers resumed their normal behavior. Although this study was intended to be a simulation of interactions between depressed mothers and infants, it is possible that infants of naturally depressed mothers may be accustomed to their mothers' behavior and may behave very differently. Thus, a follow-up to this study was conducted in which infants of naturally depressed mothers (postpartum depression) were compared to infants of nondepressed mothers who were invited to "look depressed" (Field, 1984).

In this study, the Beck Depression Inventory (Beck, Ward, Mendelson, Mock, and Erbaugh, 1961) was used to identify mothers experiencing postpartum depression (Field, 1984). The face-to-face interactions of these "depressed" mothers and their infants were then compared to the interactions of nondepressed mothers and their infants. In addition, the infants' and mothers' baseline and interaction heart rates were recorded, and an actometer was attached to the infant for a measure of activity level. Three face-to-face play interactions were recorded, including a spontaneous interaction, an interaction in which the mother was asked to "look depressed," and a "reunion" interaction in which the mother was again asked to behave naturally.

During the "looking depressed" situation (versus the spontaneous interaction), the infants of nondepressed mothers (versus those of depressed mothers) were more disturbed, showing more frequent negative facial expressions, protests, and looking-wary behavior, and higher activity levels and heart rate (see Table 2). Thus, the request to "look depressed" significantly altered the behavior of nondepressed mothers and their infants, but the behavior of naturally depressed mothers and their infants was not affected by this manipulation.

The data on the nondepressed mothers and their infants support those of Cohn and Tronick (1983), suggesting that these infants noticed

Table 2. Infant and Mother Behaviors During Spontaneous, "Depressed," and "Reunion" Interactions [Mean (M), Repeated Measures (R), and Interaction (I) Effects]*

Behaviors	Nondepressed			Depressed			Effect and p Level
	Spontaneous	Depressed	Reunion	Spontaneous	Depressed	Reunion	
Infant Behaviors							
Positive facial expressions (frequency)	8.5_a	4.0_b	4.5_b	3.0_c	2.0_c	2.0_c	M^1I^1
Negative facial expressions (frequency)	1.5_a	8.0_b	6.5_b	5.5_b	5.0_b	4.5_b	I^1
Vocalizations (frequency)	7.0_a	3.0_b	3.5_b	2.0_c	1.5_c	1.5_c	M^2I^1
Looking away (% time)	21_a	48_b	39_b	38_b	32_b	33_b	I^2
Protesting (% time)	5_a	42_b	37_b	15_c	16_c	17_c	M^2I^4
Looking wary (% time)	7_a	36_b	31_b	11_c	14_c	13_c	M^3I^4
Activity	17_a	26_b	23_b	9_c	11_c	12_c	M^2I^1
Heart rate	148_a	159_b	154_b	140_a	142_a	145_a	M^1I^1
Mother Behaviors							
Positive facial expressions (frequency)	21.5_a	2.0_b	16.5_a	5.0_b	4.0_b	3.5_b	M^3I^4
Negative facial expressions (frequency)	2.5_a	8.0_b	3.0_a	9.0_b	11.5_b	10.5_b	M^1I^1
Vocalizations (frequency)	53_a	21_b	48_a	22_b	26_b	27_b	M^2I^2
Looking at infant (% time)	93_a	89_a	95_a	58_b	65_b	62_b	M^3
Tactile/Kinesthetic stimulation (% time)	39_a	11_b	33_a	21_c	11_b	18_c	M^2R^2
Heart rate	79_a	87_b	81_a	71_c	73_c	74_c	M^1I^1

*Means bearing different subscripts (a, b, c) are different at $p < .05$ or less; SDs can be obtained from the author.

[1] $p < .05$ [3] $p < .005$
[2] $p < .01$ [4] $p < .001$

the change in their mothers' affect and modified their own affective behavior in response to their mothers "looking depressed." As in the Cohn and Tronick study, much of the infants' behavior appeared to be an attempt to reinstate a normal interaction; failing this, their distressed behavior (looking away, looking wary, and protesting) carried over into their subsequent "reunion" interaction. These data indicate a carryover of affective behavior or the establishment of a "mood" in the infant. That this may be an anxiety-provoking situation for both the nondepressed mothers and their infants is suggested by their elevated activity level and corresponding increases in heart rate during the "looking depressed" interaction.

In contrast, the naturally depressed mothers' behaviors did not appear to change across the three situations. Paralleling the unchanging behavior of the depressed mothers was the unchanging behavior of their infants. The infants of naturally depressed mothers behaved less positively during the spontaneous interaction and showed little change during the "looking depressed" interaction. These data confirm the speculation that infants of naturally depressed mothers may be accustomed to their mothers' depressed behavior and thus may not act distressed when she is invited to "look depressed." The lower heart rate of the depressed mothers and their infants may be mediated by somatic coupling of activity and heart rate (Obtrist, 1981). As we have mentioned, lower heart rate has also been associated with situations of helplessness or passive coping (Obrist, Lawler, Howard, Smithson, Martin, and Manning, 1974) and has been attributed to decreased sympathetic adrenergic activity or increased parasympathetic activation or vagal tone (McCabe and Schneiderman, 1985).

These data are reminiscent of infant primate studies in which infants do or do not have control in stressful situations (Reite, Short, Seiler, and Pauley, 1981). During brief periods of stress, infant monkeys typically show agitated behavior and physiological arousal. During more prolonged stress, their activity and physiology were depressed. In the former situation, the primate infant has been said to be actively coping and, in the latter, passively coping. The behavior of the infants of depressed mothers versus those of nondepressed mothers in this study suggests a passive-active-coping behavior contrast. The behavior of the infants of depressed mothers appeared to "mirror" the behavior of their mothers; this suggests that, by experiencing frequent lack of control during early interactions, these infants may have developed a passive-coping, depressed style of interacting. Their "depressed mood" persisted across interactions and may be a well-established "defensive posture" that would appear in situations regardless of the stimulation provided.

Very little is known about the genetic transmission of depression in families, and genetic susceptibility cannot be ruled out as a possible origin of this behavior, particularly in light of the Sameroff and Seifer (1983) data suggesting that infants of depressed mothers are at unusually high risk for developing depression. An alternative interpretation is that depressed affect may emerge in very young infants as a function of their early interactions with postpartum-depressed mothers. Whether the depressed affect of these infants derives from their "mirroring" their mothers' behaviors or simply results from minimal stimulation provided by the mothers is an empirical question. Nonetheless, these data suggest that depression in the mother may be transmitted to her offspring during their very early interactions.

Still another possibility is that these infants were "depressed" prior to experiencing early interactions with their mothers. In another study of this kind, mothers who were experiencing postpartum depression but who had also been identified during pregnancy ultrasound examination as being depressed prepartum were filmed interacting with their infants (Field, Sandberg, Garcia, Vega-Lahr, Goldstein, and Guy, 1985). Following delivery, their neonates were given a Brazelton Neonatal Assessment (Brazelton, 1973) and were noted to have "depressed" activity levels and responsivity to social stimulation, not unlike infants of mothers with elevated monoamine oxidase levels (Sostek, Sostek, Murphy, Martin, and Born, 1981). At three months postdelivery, the mothers who had been depressed during pregnancy received scores meeting the criterion for depression on the Beck depression inventory and showed flat affect and lower activity levels as well as less contingent responsivity during their interactions with their infants (see Table 3). Their infants showed fewer contented expressions and more fussiness as compared to a control group of infants of nondepressed mothers. Thus, it is not clear whether the infants' diminished activity level and responsivity during their three-month interactions were merely a behavioral style that persisted from birth, or one that largely developed from prolonged exposure to the depressed behavior modeled by their mothers, from minimal stimulation provided by their mothers, and from the infants' repeated failure to reinstate normal interactions (Tronick, Ricks, and Cohn, 1982).

A more intensive longitudinal study across pregnancy and early infancy would be required to assess the origins of this "depressed" behavior in young infants, and a comparison of the infants' behaviors during interactions with their own mothers versus other mothers might indicate whether the depressed affect of these infants is specific to interactions with depressed adults or whether they have already developed a "depressed" style of interacting. Nonetheless, the importance of studying the effects of maternal depression on infant affect is highlighted simply by the incidence of the problem, ranging from 10 to 12 percent for postpartum depression and 40 to 70 percent for postpartum blues, with residual effects after one year in approximately 4 percent of mothers and a recurrence rate reported between 20 and 30 percent (Davidson, 1972; Grundy and Roberts, 1975).

Table 3. Mean Rating Scale Scores and p Levels
Based on Bonferroni t tests (df = 23)

Behaviors	Depressed	Control	p Level
Infant Interaction Behaviors			
State	1.5	2.6	.01
Physical activity	1.6	2.5	.01
Head orientation	2.0	2.2	n.s.
Gaze behavior	2.1	2.3	n.s.
Facial expressions	1.4	2.1	.05
Vocalizations	1.5	1.6	n.s.
Fussiness	1.3	2.2	.01
Summary rating	1.6	2.2	.05
Mother Interaction Behaviors			
State	1.6	2.4	.05
Physical activity	1.8	2.7	.01
Head orientation	2.4	2.5	n.s.
Gaze behavior	2.3	2.5	n.s.
Silence during infant gaze aversion	1.5	1.3	n.s.
Imitative behaviors	1.4	2.2	.05
Contingent responsivity	1.5	2.3	.05
Gameplaying	1.4	2.2	.05
Summary rating	1.7	2.3	.05
Questionnaire Ratings			
CCTI-emotionality	20	13	.01
EASI-emotionality	18	12	.01
Childrearing attitudes	05	01	.05
Locus of control	28	15	.01
State anxiety	38	29	.05
Trait anxiety	51	28	.01
Beck depression	22	04	.01

Summary

The infant's responsivity (both behavioral and physiological) develops in the context of an interactive relationship with the mother (caregiver). The mother serves as a modulator in providing adequate stimulation, arousal modulation, and the kind of regulation needed for the development of organized behavioral patterns and physiological rhythms. If the mother (caregiver) is affectively unavailable or unresponsive (as in the depressed mother), or if the infant is separated from the mother, behavioral and physiological disorganization will invariably ensue, manifested by disturbances in affective and/or vegetative functions. We believe that the depressed mother may predispose the infant to chronic depression and that the separation situation may provide a model for reactive depression.

References

Ainsworth, M. D. *Infancy in Uganda*. Baltimore, Md.: John Hopkins University Press, 1967.
Bakeman, R., and Brown, J. "Early Interaction: Consequences for Social and Mental Development at Three Years." *Child Development*, 1980, *51*, 437-447.
Beck, A. T., Ward, C. H., Mendelson, M., Mock, J. E., and Erbaugh, J. "An Inventory for Measuring Depression." *Archives of General Psychiatry*, 1961, *4*, 561-571.
Bowlby, J. *Attachment and Loss, Vol. 1: Attachment*. New York: Basic Books, 1969.
Brazelton, T. B. *Neonatal Behavioral Assessment Scale*. London: Spastic International Medical Publications, 1973.
Breese, G. R., Smith, R. D., Mueller, R. A., Howard, J. L., Prange, A. J., Lipton, M. A., Young, L. D., McKinney, W. T., and Lewis, J. K. "Induction of Adrenal Catecholamine Synthesizing Enzymes Following Mother-Infant Separation." *Nature, New Biology*, 1973, *246*, 94-96.
Clarke-Stewart, K. A. "And Daddy Makes Three: The Father's Impact on Mother and Child." *Child Development*, 1978, *49*, 466-478.
Cohn J. F., and Tronick, E. Z. "Three-Month-Old Infants' Reaction to Simulated Maternal Depression." *Child Development*, 1983, *54*, 185-193.
Cytryn, L., McKnew, D. H., Bartko, J. J., Lamour, M., and Hamovitt, J. "Offspring of Patients with Affective Disorders." *Journal of American Academy of Child Psychiatry*, 1982, *21*, 389-391.
Davidson, J. R. "Postpartum Mood Changes in Jamaican Women." *British Journal of Psychiatry*, 1972, *121*, 659-663.
Emde, R. N., Harmon, R. J., Metcalf, D., Koenig, K. L., and Wagonfeld, S. "Stress and Neonatal Sleep." *Psychosomatic Medicine*, 1971, *33*, 491-497.
Engel, G. L., and Schmale, A. H. "Conservation-Withdrawal: A Primary Regulatory Process for Organismic Homeostasis." In Ciba Foundation Symposium 8, *Physiology, Emotion, and Psychosomatic Illness*. Amsterdam: Elsevier, 1972.
Field, T. "Interaction Behaviors of Primary Versus Secondary Caretaker Fathers." *Developmental Psychology*, 1978, *14* (2), 183-184.
Field, T. "Fathers' Interactions with Their High-Risk Infants." *Infant Mental Health Journal*, 1981, *2*, 249-256.
Field, T. "Early Interactions Between Infants and Their Postpartum Depressed Mothers." *Infant Behavior and Development*, 1984, *7*, 527-532.

Field, T. "Affective Response to Separation." In T. B. Brazelton and M. W. Yogman (eds.), *Affective Development in Infancy.* Norwood, N.J.: Ablex, 1985.

Field, T., Dempsey, J., and Shuman, H. H. "Five-Year Follow-Up of Preterm Respiratory Distress Syndrome and Postterm Postmaturity Syndrome Infants." In T. Field and A Sostek (eds.), *Infants Born at Risk: Physiological, Perceptual, and Cognitive Processes.* New York: Grune & Stratton, 1983.

Field, T., Sandberg, D., Garcia, R., Vega-Lahr, N., Goldstein, S., and Guy, L. "Prenatal Problems, Postpartum Depression, and Early Mother-Infant Interactions." *Developmental Psychology,* 1985, *12,* 1152-1156.

Grundy, P. F., and Roberts, C. J. "Observations on the Epidemiology of Postpartum Mental Illness." *Psychosomatic Medicine,* 1975, *53,* 286-290.

Harlow, H. F., and Harlow, M. K. "The Affectional Systems." In A. M. Schrier, H. F. Harlow, and F. Stollnitz (eds.), *Behavior of Nonhuman Primates.* Vol. 2. New York: Academic Press, 1965.

Lamb, M. E. "Fathers: Forgotten Contributors to Child Development." *Human Development,* 1975, *18,* 245-266.

Legg, C., Sherick, I., and Wadland, W. "Reaction of Preschool Children to the Birth of a Sibling." *Child Psychiatry and Human Development,* 1974, *5,* 3-59.

Levine, S., and Coe, C. L. "The Use and Abuse of Cortisol as a Measure of Stress." In T. Field, P. McCabe, and N. Schneiderman (eds.), *Stress and Coping.* Vol. 2. Hillsdale, N.J.: Erlbaum, 1985.

McCabe, P., and Schneiderman, N. "Psychophysiological Reactions to Stress." In N. Schneiderman and J. Tapp (eds.), *Behavioral Medicine: The Biopsychosocial Approach.* Hillsdale, N.J.: Erlbaum, 1985.

Obrist, P. A. *Cardiovascular Psychophysiology.* New York: Plenum, 1981.

Obrist, P. A., Lawler, J. E., Howard, J. L., Smithson, K. W., Martin, P. L., and Manning, J. "Sympathetic Influences on Cardiac Rate and Contractility During Acute Stress in Humans." *Psychophysiology,* 1974, *11,* 405-427.

Parke, R. "Perspectives on Father-Infant Interaction." In J. D. Osofsky (ed.), *Handbook of Infancy.* New York: Wiley, 1979.

Reite, M. "Development of Attachment and Depression." Paper presented at the biennial meeting of the Society for Research in Child Development, Detroit, Michigan, April 1983.

Reite, M., Short, R., Kaufman, I. C., Stynes, A. J., and Pauley, J. D. "Heart Rate and Body Temperature in Separated Monkey Infants." *Biological Psychiatry,* 1978, *13,* 91-105.

Reite, M., Short, R., Seiler, C., and Pauley, J. D. "Attachment, Loss, and Depression." *Journal of Child Psychology and Psychiatry,* 1981, *22,* 141-169.

Reite, M., and Snyder, D. S. "Physiology of Maternal Separation in a Bonnet Macaque Infant." *American Journal of Primatology,* 1982, *2,* 115-120.

Robertson, J., and Robertson, J. "Young Children in Brief Separation." *Psychoanalytic Study of the Child,* 1971, *26,* 264-315.

Sameroff, A. V., and Seifer, R., "Familial Risk and Child Competence." *Child Development,* 1983, *54,* 1254-1268.

Seiler, C., Cullen, J. S., Zimmerman, J., and Reite, M. "Cardiac Arrhythmias in Infant Pigtail Monkeys Following Maternal Separation." *Psychophysiology,* 1979, *16,* 103-135.

Sostek, A. J., Sostek, A. M., Murphy, D. L., Martin, E. B., and Born, W. S. "Cord Blood Amine Oxidase Activities Relate to Arousal and Motor Functioning in Human Newborns." *Life Science,* 1981, *28* (22), 2561-2568.

Spitz, R. "Anaclitic Depression." *Psychoanalytic Study of the Child,* 1946, *2,* 113-117.

Suomi, S. J., Collins, J. L., and Harlow, H. F. "Effects of Maternal and Peer Separations on Young Monkeys." *Journal of Child Psychology and Psychiatry*, 1976, *17*, 101-112.

Tronick, E., Als, H., Adamson, L., Wise, S., and Brazelton, T. B. "The Infant's Response to Entrapment Between Contradictory Messages in Face-to-Face Interaction." *Journal of Child Psychiatry*, 1977, *17*, 1-13.

Tronick, E., Ricks, M., and Cohn, J. "Maternal and Infant Affective Exchange: Patterns of Adaptation." In T. Field and A. Fogel (eds.), *Emotion and Early Interactions*. Hillsdale, N.J.: Erlbaum, 1982.

Yogman, M. W. "Games Fathers and Mothers Play with Their Infants." *Infant Mental Health Journal*, 1981, *2*, 241-248.

Tiffany Field is professor of pediatrics and psychology at the Mailman Center for Child Development, University of Miami Medical School. Her research has focused on affective development and disorders in infants and young children.

Maternal depression is a prevalent symptom among low-income mothers with infants. Depressed mothers are more likely than nondepressed mothers to show hostile and intrusive behavior toward their infants, and infants of depressed mothers are more likely to exhibit slowed development and unstable, avoidant attachment behaviors.

The Depressed Mother and Her One-Year-Old Infant: Environment, Interaction, Attachment, and Infant Development

Karlen Lyons-Ruth, David Zoll, David Connell, Henry U. Grunebaum

Evidence is accumulating that maternal depression is a potent risk factor for childhood psychopathology. The Rochester study (Fisher, Harder, and Kokes, 1980; Kokes, Harder, Fisher, and Strauss, 1980) of latency-aged sons of psychiatrically hospitalized parents found that children of neurotically depressed parents were functioning as poorly as children of schizophrenic parents, with both groups significantly impaired compared to matched controls (children of healthy parents). Unexpectedly, children of manic-depressive parents were doing as well as the controls. The results indicated that the most important influences on the child's adjustment were the overall level of maternal functioning in the home and the availability of

---

This study was supported by National Institute of Mental Health (NIMH) Grant Number 355122 awarded to Karlen Lyons-Ruth and Henry U. Grunebaum.

maternal affect, rather than more specific psychiatric variables such as diagnostic label, presence or severity of psychotic symptoms, or length of hospitalization. The father's level of impairment was not strongly related to childhood adjustment.

Other studies have found children of unipolar, psychotically depressed mothers to be the most impaired group when compared to children of schizophrenic mothers and to controls (Grunebaum, Cohler, Kauffman, and Gallant, 1978; Rolf, Crowther, Teri, and Bond, 1984). While all of the depressed mothers in these studies had been hospitalized, a review of the epidemiological literature by Boyd and Weissman (1981) reveals that between 20 and 26 percent of women in the general community experience major depression during their lifetimes, and only about a quarter of these women ever receive psychiatric treatment (Weissman, Myers, and Thompson, 1981).

Similarly, in our clinical experience, we have found a large number of very depressed women living in inner-city neighborhoods with no history of contact with any mental health agency. Brown and Harris (1975), in their careful epidemiological study, found that the incidence of major depression among women was related to the extent of economic hardship, to the presence of a child under six, and to the absence of a close family member as a confidant. Furthermore, they found that these risk factors in combination had multiplicative rather than additive effects on the numbers of depressed women. Interestingly, the greater vulnerability of working-class women to depression was true only among women with children living at home. Thus, while this volume focuses on the effects of maternal depression on the child, Brown and Harris's data emphasize the transactional nature of the system, since the presence of the child affects the mother and her susceptibility to depression.

In one of the most comprehensive community surveys of childhood psychopathology, Rutter and colleagues (1975) identified six family variables that were associated with increased incidence of psychopathology in latency-aged children. These were marital discord and disruption, low socioeconomic status (SES), maternal symptoms of anxiety and depression, paternal criminality, large family size, and placement of the child into foster care.

Rutter (1979) also found that the presence of a single risk factor did not produce an increase in childhood disorder. However, the presence of two risk factors increased the proportion of disturbed children fourfold, and three or four concurrent stresses further multiplied the incidence of disorder. Thus, the addition of risk factors resulted in multiplicative rather than additive effects on the number of disturbed children.

Rutter's extensive epidemiological data confirm the significance of maternal neurotic depression and anxiety as one of the six family factors associated with increased incidence of childhood psychopathology. His data places the role of maternal psychiatric disorder in a larger context, however, in pointing out that childhood disorder is not predicted by the presence of a single risk factor. Instead, multiple stressors are necessary, and maternal depression is a frequent but not a necessary ingredient of the multistress environments leading to childhood psychological disorder.

The potency of low socioeconomic status as a contributor to various poor developmental outcomes, including psychopathology, learning disabilities, and school failure, has been confirmed in most studies that have included socioeconomic status as a variable (Broman, Nichols, and Kennedy, 1975; Rutter and others, 1975; Sameroff and Chandler, 1975). Sameroff, Seifer, and Zax (1982), in a study of infants of previously psychiatrically hospitalized mothers, concluded that the deleterious effects of low socioeconomic status were more striking than effects associated with the psychiatric diagnosis itself.

Given these data, keep in mind that this chapter describes the correlates of depression in the context of very low socioeconomic status. Maternal depression in more advantaged groups is not only less prevalent (Dohrenwend and Dohrenwend, 1969) but may also have somewhat different correlates than maternal depression in the context of other concurrent risk factors such as low SES.

The data reported in this chapter were gathered as part of a clinical research project designed to investigate the impact of social risk factors and the provision of preventive services on infant development in a very low income, inner-city population. A major goal of the study was to refine our understanding of the processes mediating the linkage between low SES and childhood psychopathology, with the assumption that all infants in low-income families are not equally at risk.

The focus of this chapter is on whether maternal depression is a risk factor for infant development, as well as for childhood psychopathology, and whether maternal behaviors can be identified that mediate relationships between maternal depression and infant developmental outcome. Three specific questions will be addressed:

1. What proportion of the group of multirisk mothers with infants referred for clinical intervention services can be characterized as suffering from depression? Or is maternal depression not a frequent characteristic of the most at-risk mother-infant dyads?

2. What is the ecological context of maternal depression in this sample? How does depression relate to the mother's past and present family context?

3. How does the mother's depression affect her maternal behavior and her infant's development and security of attachment at twelve months of age?

Methods

Characteristics of the High-Risk and Community Samples. One-half of our sample of mothers and infants was referred to a clinical infant intervention service because of a poor mother-infant relationship and economic and social stresses within the family. Maternal depression itself was not the criterion for referral. Infants were between zero and nine months of age at referral.

This clinically referred high-risk sample was individually matched with a community sample of mothers and infants drawn from the same neighborhoods who had never sought or received social services directed at parenting skills and had never undergone psychiatric hospitalization. The high-risk and community groups were individually matched on per-person family income, mother's education and race, and the child's age, sex, and birth order (firstborn or laterborn). Analysis by Chi-square of F test confirmed that the high-risk and community groups did not differ on any of the six matching variables or on infant birthweight, mother's age at birth of child, or mean number of siblings.

Further Information on Methods. The complete design of the intervention portion of the investigation and the complete list of assessment measures can be found in Lyons-Ruth, Connell, Grunebaum, Botein, and Zoll (1984). A detailed description of the two clinical service models and of the clinical issues that arose in working with these highly stressed families is presented in Lyons-Ruth, Botein, and Grunebaum (1984). Mother-infant interaction and attachment data for the maltreating subgroup in the current sample are presented in detail by Lyons-Ruth, Connell, Zoll, and Stahl (in press).

Assessment Procedures

Assessment of Maternal Depression. Maternal depression was assessed by the Center for Epidemiological Studies Depression Scale (CES-D), which is a twenty-item, sixty-point questionnaire asking about depressive symptoms during the past week (Radloff, 1977). It has been well validated in large-scale epidemiological studies, with 99 percent of patients with known depression scoring above 16 (Weissman and others, 1977). The cutoff point of 16 also differentiates well in unselected community groups between depressed and nondepressed people, with a false-positive rate of 6.1 percent and a false-negative rate of 36.4 percent (Myers and Weissman, 1980). Eighty to 91 percent of the population score below 16 (Comstock and Helsing, 1976; Husaini and others, 1980).

The depression scale was administered twice in interviews with the mother at home—once when the family entered the study (at an infant age of birth to twelve months) and once when the infants reached eighteen months of age.

Assessment of Maternal Family History. A maternal family history interview was conducted at the mother's home at study entry. Family history information was gathered in two parts. First, the mother, was asked to trace all changes in adult caregivers from her birth to age sixteen. Additional questions were asked about the incidence of psychiatric hospitalization, drug or alcohol abuse, or time in prison of adults within the mother's family of origin. The occupational levels of both of the mother's parents were rated on the nine-point Occupational Scale from the Hollingshead (1975) Four-Factor Index of Social Status.

The second part of the family history interview consisted of thirty-five structured items probing five domains of early life experience hypothesized to relate to the mother's social adjustment and mothering capacities, including family warmth, conflict, and structure, and peer and school experiences. Internal consistency for the five qualitative family history scales, assessed by Cronbach's *Alpha* (1951) ranged from .56 to .74.

Assessment of Maternal Behavior at Home. Naturalistic mother-infant interaction was videotaped at home for forty minutes when the infants were twelve months of age. Mothers were told that the observer was interested in recording a typical segment of the infant's day and asked to conduct themselves as they usually would. Maternal behavior was coded in ten four-minute intervals on twelve five-point rating scales and one timed variable. These included Sensitivity, Warmth, Verbal Communication, Quality and Quantity of Relational Touching (physical contact in the service of communicating affection, "touching base," or reducing distress), Quality and Quantity of Caretaking Touching, Interfering Manipulation, Covert Hostility, Anger, Disengagement, Flatness of Affect, and Time Out of the Room, rounded to the nearest half-minute. Coders were blind to other information on the families, and all ratings were reliable. Methodological details are presented by Lyons-Ruth, Connell, Zoll, and Stahl (in press).

Infant behavior at home is being coded separately and is not yet available for analysis.

Assessment of Infant Development. The Bayley Scales of Infant Development, Mental, and Motor Scales (Bayley, 1969), were administered to each infant in a laboratory visit at twelve months of age. The Bayley Scales were administered before assessment in the Ainsworth Strange Situation (Ainsworth, Blehar, Waters, and Wall, 1978).

Assessment of Maternal Intelligence. To provide an estimate of maternal intelligence, the Similarities subscale of the Wechsler Adult Intelligence Scale (WAIS), 1955 edition, was administered as part of the twelve-month laboratory visit. This subscale had a reliability coefficient of .85 and correlated highly with both Full-Scale IQ scores ($r = .79$) and Verbal scores ($r = .83$) in the WAIS standardization sample (Wechsler, 1955).

Assessment of Infant Attachment Security. Within two weeks of home videotaping, mothers and infants were videotaped in the Ainsworth Strange

Situation. In this procedure, the infant is videotaped in a playroom during a series of eight structured three-minute episodes involving the baby, the mother, and a female stranger. During the observation, the mother leaves and rejoins the infant twice, first leaving the infant with the female stranger, then leaving the infant alone. The procedure is designed to be mildly stressful in order to increase the intensity of activation of the infant's attachment behavior. All videotapes were coded as described by Ainsworth, Blehar, Waters, and Wall (1978). Coders were blind to all other data on the families, including high-risk status. Reliability coefficients for individual variables computed on independent coding of 20 percent of the tapes ranged from .97 to .72, with a mean of .86 (all $p < .01$). Further methodological details are presented by Lyons-Ruth, Connell, Zoll, and Stahl (in press).

Methodological Issues. The depression data, almost by definition, have a somewhat skewed distribution. Therefore, all analyses were computed both by linear and by rank-order methods to check on the stability of the linear results. We were particularly concerned that the few very high scores might create spurious effects in a linear analysis—effects that would not represent the sample as a whole. However, the two methods yielded very similar results. Contrary to our concerns, the linear analyses never produced significant results that were not also confirmed by the rank-order method. Given the power, flexibility, and robustness of linear analytic tools, we suggest that they be retained for analysis of data from extreme populations but that checking procedures be instituted. The simultaneous use of nonlinear methods, data transformation, or reanalysis after removal of extreme scores can help assess the stability of the findings.

Results

Stability of Maternal Depression in a Low-Income Sample. Maternal depression assessed at the beginning and end of the study (a six-to eighteen-month interval) was remarkably stable in this low-income sample ($r = .73$). Only nine mothers changed from the depressed to the nondepressed group or vice versa over the time period of the study, and those changes were evenly balanced between increased and decreased depression. As would be expected, the rate of maternal depression was higher in this sample than in the general population. At study intake, 52.4 percent of the mothers reported depressive symptoms above the cutoff point of 16, with a similar proportion, 54.6 percent, scoring above the cutoff point when the infants were eighteen months old. Due to the similarities in the intake and termination depression scores, the initial scores only will be used in the rest of this chapter. For the four mothers with missing intake scores, the termination scores were substituted.

Maternal Depression and Clinical Provider Judgments of High-Risk Status. Maternal depression as assessed by the CES-D scale proved to be strongly associated with high-risk status in this study ($F(1,54) = 12.16$, $p < .001$), even though depression was not explicitly singled out in discussions with pediatric and social service providers as an indicator for referral. Almost two-thirds of high-risk mothers (64 percent) but only one-third of community group mothers (29 percent) reported depressive symptoms above the cutoff point of 16 established in previous epidemiological research as indicating a clinical case of depression (Comstock and Helsing, 1976; Husaini and others, 1980; Myers and Weissman, 1980). Means for the two groups were 23.18 and 12.39, respectively. The community group mean is somewhat higher than the mean of 9.70 for very low income rural community respondents reported by Husaini and others (1980), but the incidence of depression in the community group (29 percent) is similar to the incidence of depression among working-class women with a child under six (31 percent), as reported in the epidemiological study of Brown and Harris (1975).

Despite this high rate of depression in the sample, depression was not an obvious aspect of many mothers' presentations to care providers. Rather, nurses or social workers observed neglect, apathy, or anger in the mother's response to her infant, or excessive worries about the infant's health, with overuse of medical services. Other mothers were referred because of the involvement of protective services or because of serious infant symptoms such as failure to thrive. Depressive symptoms were more directly involved as a reason for referral only for those mothers who had been psychiatrically hospitalized for depression, and, in those cases, the hospitalization, rather than the type of symptom that led to the hospitalization, was the basis for referral. Mothers were also hospitalized for schizophrenia, alcoholism, conversion reactions, and brief psychotic episodes.

Given the many disparate presenting problems for these mother-infant dyads, the high frequency with which maternal depression was an underlying part of the picture was unexpected. It suggests that the contribution of maternal depression to childhood psychopathology may cut across conventional diagnostic categories. The prevalence of maternal depression among the most-at-risk group of mothers and infants provides a compelling reason to further our understanding of the context and developmental effects of this maternal symptom.

Maternal Depression and Maternal Psychiatric Hospitalization. Mothers who had been psychiatrically hospitalized gave the highest mean CES-D score of any subgroup in the data, further validating the CES-D reports [$F(1, 54) = 8.00$, $p < .006$]. Previously hospitalized mothers earned a mean score of 28.11 on the CES-D, well over the cutoff point of 16, while the rest of the sample earned a mean of 15.80. Seventy-eight percent of previously hospitalized mothers scored above the cutoff point of 16, and 56 percent earned scores over 30, compared to 40 percent and 13 percent, respectively, for the rest of the sample. Thus, severe depressive symptoms were very prominent among the hospitalized mothers in our sample.

Mothers who were hospitalized for anxiety disorders and alcoholism as well as for major depression reported severe depression on the CES-D. Mothers with psychotic symptoms, particularly paranoid ideation, were much less likely to report depressive feelings (see also Myers and Weissman, 1980). However, these mothers are both less frequent in the psychiatric population and less likely to maintain custody of their infants among a poor, often single-parent population.

Maternal Depression and Demographic Data. One might not expect demographic variables (such as socioeconomic status) that have been correlated with maternal depression in large-scale epidemiologic studies (for example, Brown and Harris, 1975) to remain correlated in the present sample due to the narrow economic range in the sample and to the matching procedures employed. To the extent that maternal depression was related to referral into the high-risk group, the matching of those families with community comparison families on infant age, sex, and birth order and on maternal race, education, and family income would also have acted to attenuate the relationships between these demographic variables and maternal depression. Despite this effect of the matching process, relationships similar to those reported by Brown and Harris (1975) between maternal depression and lower SES and between maternal depression and number of children in the home were also evident in our sample, as shown in Table 1.

Within this low-income sample, maternal depression was significantly more severe and more frequent for mothers supported by Aid to Families of Dependent Children (AFDC) than for other mothers. This was not simply a function of the absence of a male companion in the homes of AFDC mothers, nor was it related to a difference in level of income between AFDC and non-AFDC families. Neither presence of the father in the home nor income level related reliably to maternal depression in itself. Families supported by male employment were not significantly better off financially than AFDC families, and male partners in the home were often not a source of financial or emotional support, since there was a relatively high frequency of male violence, drug or alcohol abuse, and nonsupport in the study sample. Thus, the relationship between maternal depression and welfare support must reflect other factors than low income level or absence of a male partner.

Also consistent with the findings of Brown and Harris (1975), mothers with more than one child reported more severe depressive symptoms than mothers with only one infant. The Chi-square test for simple presence or absence of depression by number of children was not significant in this sample, however, probably due to the attenuating effect of matching high-risk and comparison samples on birth order. These data are also presented in Table 1.

Table 1. Maternal Depression and Current and Past Family Characteristics

Current Family Characteristics	Variables Associated with Severity of Maternal Depression[a, b]	Variables Associated with Presence or Absence of Maternal Depression[a, b] (CES-D ≥ 16)
Family receiving government assistance	$F(1,54) = 5.73$[c]	$X^2(1, n = 56) = 7.65$[d]
Birth order of infant (first born or not)	$F(1,54) = 2.94$[e]	NS
Mother's age at birth of child	Not significant (NS)	NS
Male companion in home	NS	NS
Presence of abuse or neglect	NS	NS
Occupational level of family wage earner (Hollingshead scale)	NS	NS
Mother's race (white, nonwhite)	NS	NS
Mother's education (high school graduate or not)	NS	NS
Per-person weekly income	NS	NS
Sex of infant	NS	NS
Family History Information[f]		
Quality of parental warmth	$r = -.43$[a]	$F(1,54) = 14.11$[a]
Quality of peer friendships	$r = -.39$[d]	$F(1,54) = 2.99$[e]
Lack of family conflict	$r = -.37$[d]	$F(1,54) = 12.34$[a]
Lack of psychopathology among family members	$r = -.32$[d]	$F(1,54) = 4.91$[c]
Lack of maternal psychopathology	$F(1,54) = 4.67$[c]	$X^1(1, n = 56) = 3.66$[c]
Lack of paternal psychopathology	NS	NS
Quality of school experience	$r = -.20$[e]	NS
Quality of structure and supervision	NS	NS
Parents' occupational level (Hollingshead scale)	$r = -.28$[c]	NS
Number of times family moved ($N = 55$)	$r = -.24$[c]	NS
Stable two-parent family versus nonintact family (foster care group excluded) ($N = 45$)	NS	NS
Spent time in foster care as child versus no foster care	$F(1,54) = 4.59$[c]	NS

[a] $n = 56$ unless otherwise noted.
[b] For all r or F values reported, the corresponding rank-order statistic (Kendall's Tau or Mann Whitney's U) was also significant.
[c] $p < .05$.
[d] $p < .01$.
[e] $p < .10$.
[f] In the first nine family history scales, higher scores indicate a more positive family environment.
[g] $p < .001$.

Maternal Depression and Reports of Maternal Family History. In contrast to the few current correlates of maternal depression, such depression was strongly related to the mothers' reports of their family histories before age sixteen. Mothers who reported more depressive symptoms were significantly more likely to come from families of lower occupational rank and to report less warmth in their relations with parents, more maternal (but not paternal) psychopathology (psychiatric, drug, or alcohol problems), more violence and conflict at home, more moves from residence to residence, and poorer relationships with peers and teachers. They were also more likely to have spent periods of time in foster care. These findings are also displayed in Table 1.

Because the family history variables were moderately intercorrelated, a stepwise multiple-regression procedure was performed to assess which family history variables accounted for independent portions of variance in current depression. Two of the family history variables accounted for 28 percent of the variance in current maternal depression. Parental warmth accounted for 18 percent of the variance in maternal depression and peer relationships for an independent 10 percent after parental warmth scores were factored out.

The family history variables, thus, emerged as important indicators of maternal depression in a sample in which depressed and nondepressed groups were well matched on socioeconomic status. Although data regarding the construct validity of these reports were not gathered in the current study, our data converge well with those reported by Crook, Raskin, and Eliot (1981), who were able to obtain validating family history information from friends and relatives of the depressed and control subjects. The two studies taken together indicate that the relationship between early satisfying relationships and depression holds across a wide range of depressed respondents, from psychiatric inpatients to depressed women in the community who are resistant to seeking conventional psychiatric care.

Relations Between Maternal Depression and Maternal Behavior. Several aspects of mothers' interactive behaviors toward their year-old infants were significantly related to their depression scores. Increasing maternal depression was associated with increased maternal Covert Hostility, increased Interfering Manipulation, and decreased Flatness of Affect in mother-infant interaction. Thus, higher maternal depression was related to greater affectivity, more covert hostility, and more interference with the infant's goal-directed activity (Table 2).

These findings are consistent with the findings of Weissman and Paykel (1974) and of Belle (1982) on the interactions of depressed mothers with their latency-aged and adolescent children. In contrast to the mothers' passive and withdrawn presentations to nonfamily members, depressed mothers in those studies, when observed at home, were significantly more angry and controlling toward their children than nondepressed controls.

Table 2. Significant Pearson Correlations Between Maternal Depression Scores and Maternal Behavior at Home

Maternal Behavior at Home	N:	Full Sample 56	CES-D = 0 Removed 53	CES-D = 0, 1 Removed 51	CES-D = 0, 1, 2 Removed 48	CES-D = 0, 1, 2, 5[a] Removed 46
Covert hostility		.22[b]	.34[c]	.32[c]	.30[b]	.27[b]
Interfering manipulation		.20[d]	.36[c]	.33[c]	.33[c]	.31[b]
Flatness of affect		−.23[b]	−.29[b]	−.32[c]	−.26[b]	−.24[b]

[a] No subjects in the study reported CES-D scores of 3 or 4.
[b] $p < .05$.
[c] $p < .01$.
[d] $p < .10$.

Given the relatively high false-negative rates in self-reports of depressive symptoms, one follow-up analysis was conducted to evaluate whether a subgroup of women denying their depression could be identified among those giving low CES-D scores. We first hypothesized that a score of zero on the CES-D might potentially indicate denial, so the depression by maternal behavior correlations were recalculated with these subjects removed from the data. The correlations became much stronger, as shown in Table 2. We then repeated the process with CES-D scores through five, to see at what point the removal of data ceased to improve the linear association between depression scores and maternal behavior. It is apparent from Table 2 that only the removal of data from mothers giving scores of zero substantially affected the obtained correlations. Thus, it appears that scores of zero on the CES-D are likely to be suspect and to characterize mothers whose behavior is more similar to the behavior of depressed mothers than to the behavior of nondepressed mothers. Mean behavioral scores for mothers giving scores of zero on the CES-D confirmed this impression from the correlational data. Those mothers were rated particularly high on Covert Hostility and Interfering Manipulation.

Maternal Depression and Infant Development at One Year. Maternal depression was also significantly related to the infants' scores at one year of age on the Mental Development Index (MDI) and Physical Development Index (PDI) of the Bayley Scales ($r = -.32$ and $r = -.30$, respectively). Mothers' IQ estimates from the Similarities subtest of the WAIS were also related to the infant's Mental Development scores at one year old, as were the mother's Sensitivity, Warmth, and Verbal Communication. Intercorrelations among these measures are displayed in Table 3.

In order to assess the relative contribution of maternal depression

Table 3. Maternal Behavior, IQ, and Depression and Infant Mental and Motor Development at One Year of Age

Maternal Behaviors at Home	N:	Infant MDI	Infant PDI	Maternal IQ	Maternal CES-D
		56	56	46	56
Sensitivity		.26[a]	.05	.38[b]	-.05
Warmth		.23[a]	.05	.32[a]	-.00
Verbal Communication		.25[a]	.21[c]	.17	.13
Maternal IQ		.44[d]	.23[a]	—	-.12
Maternal CES-D score		-.32[b]	-.30[b]	-.12	—

[a] $p < .05$.
[b] $p < .01$.
[c] $p < .10$.
[d] $p < .001$.

to the prediction of infant development in the context of maternal behavior and maternal IQ, a stepwise multiple-regression analysis was performed on the mental and motor development scores, with maternal depression, maternal IQ, and the three maternal behaviors as the predictor variables. IQ data were only available on forty-six of the fifty-six mothers in the twelve-month sample.

The mothers' IQ scores accounted for the most variance in infant mental development at twelve months (19.2 percent), while the severity of maternal depression accounted for an additional 11.3 percent. No other variable accounted for significant portions of variance after these two were entered. These two variables together accounted for 30.5 percent of the variance in mental development ($F(2,43) = 9.45$, $p < .0004$). In light of the developmental literature relating maternal responsiveness to enhanced mental development, we find it noteworthy that maternal IQ and maternal depression accounted for this relationship primarily due to the covariation between maternal IQ and maternal behavior as shown in Table 3.

For infant motor development, the mother's depression scores accounted for the most variance (15.9 percent), while maternal Verbal Communication accounted for an additional 9.4 percent, for a total of 25.3 percent of the variance ($F(2,43) = 7.27$, $p < .002$).

Thus, it appears that maternal depression makes an important negative contribution to infant mental and motor development during the infant's first year, accounting for 10 to 15 percent of the variance even after the effects of maternal IQ are controlled.

Figure 1 displays the mean infant mental and physical development scores for different levels of maternal depression. As is apparent from the figure, infant development scores appear to be enhanced by an absence of maternal depression, to remain at an average level even when the mothers report clinically significant levels of depression (scores of 16 to 23), and to drop again as scores exceed 32. There is also indication that infant physical development during the infant's first year may be sensitive to less severe levels of maternal depression than infant mental development.

It should be noted that mothers who deny depression on the CES Depression Scale (scores of zero) while behaving like depressed mothers during the home observation have infants whose developmental progress is average to above average, in keeping with the scores of infants whose mothers do not show depression-related behavioral patterns at home. Thus, the "denying" mothers may represent a third type of behavioral organization characterized not only by latent hostility, interfering behavior,

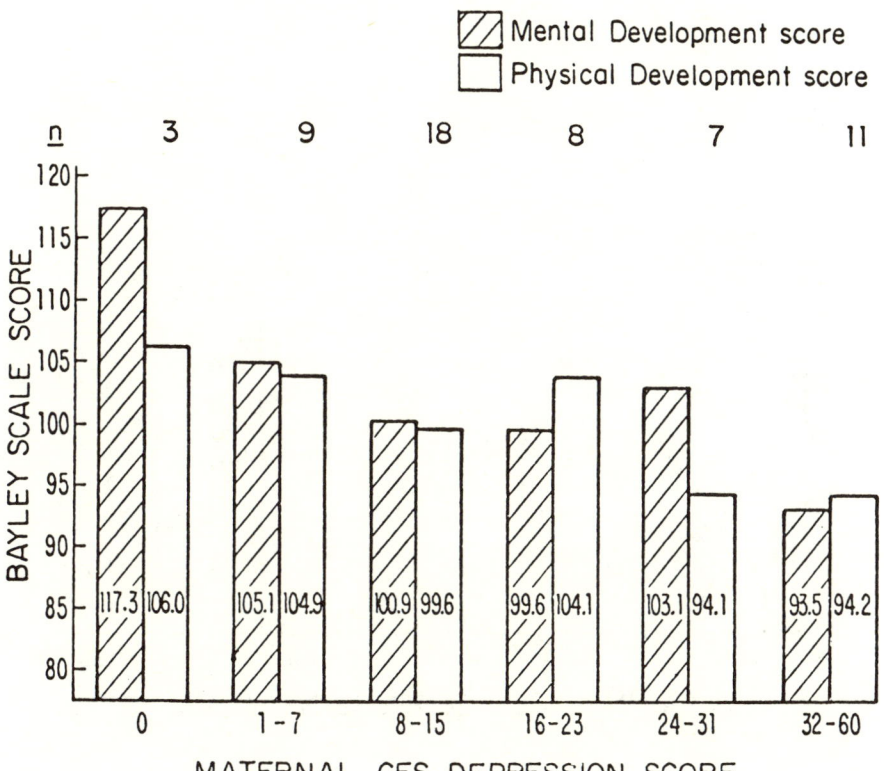

Figure 1. Infant Mental and Physical Development as a Function of Maternal Depression

and increased affectivity but also by some compensating characteristics that allow them to disavow depressed feelings and to support the developmental progress of their infants. It is also noteworthy that all these mothers were in the community comparison group. One is reminded of Mary Main's description of the rigid, obsessional mothers in Ainsworth's middle-class longitudinal sample (Ainsworth and others, 1978). These mothers appeared to be keeping angry emotions in check in interactions with their infants. This maternal pattern was associated in that sample with infant

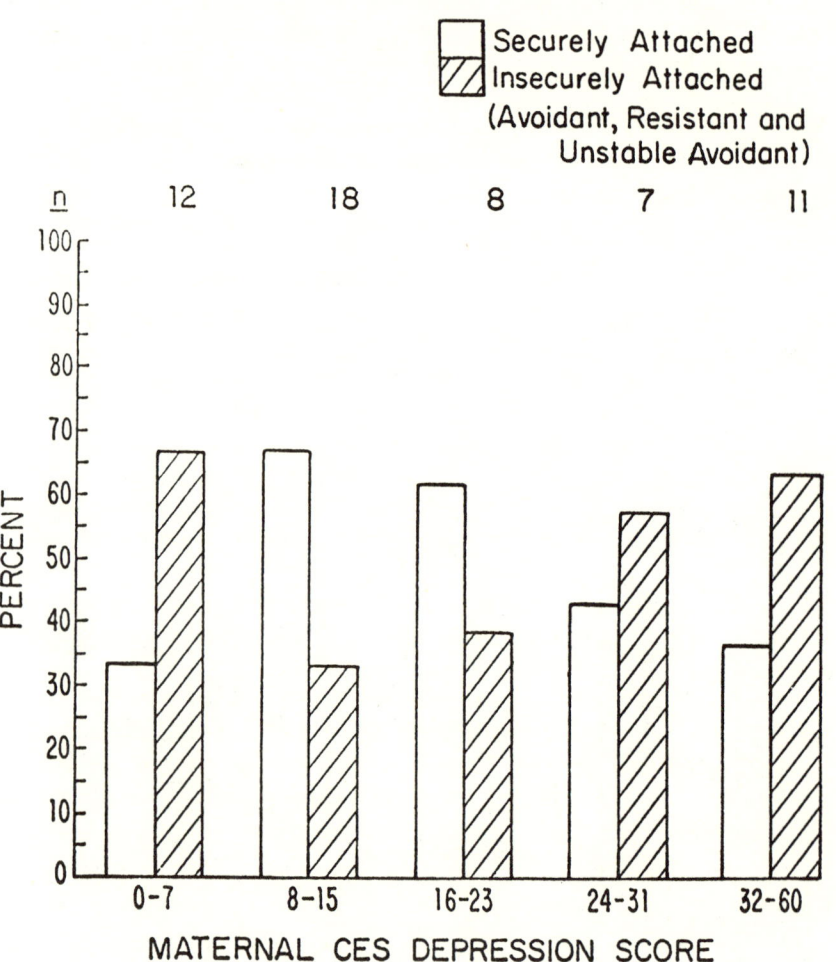

Figure 2. Maternal Depression and Secure and Insecure Attachment in Infants

avoidance of the mother in the Strange Situation but with adequate developmental scores on the Bayley Scales.

Maternal Depression and Infant Attachment. Despite the significant linear relationships between maternal depression and maternal behavior and between maternal depression and infant development, maternal depression showed no linear relation to infant attachment behavior. Depressed and nondepressed mothers did not differ in incidence of insecure infant attachment, nor did the maternal depression scores correlate with infant reunion behaviors in the Strange Situation, including infant avoidance or resistance at reunion.

When the incidence of insecure attachment was plotted by severity of maternal depression scores, as shown in Figure 2, a clearly curvilinear relationship was revealed. This curvilinear relationship between maternal depression and infant security of attachment has also been reported by Spieker and Booth (1985). Spieker and Booth, studying a similarly low-income sample, found that mothers of avoidant infants reported the lowest mean depression scores, while mothers of avoidant/resistant infants (a new classification termed A/C by these investigators) gave the highest mean depression scores, with mothers of secure infants in the middle.

Similarly, in our sample, infants whose mothers reported the least frequent depressive symptoms and infants whose mothers reported the most frequent symptoms were about equally likely to show insecure attachment. Mothers who reported mild to moderate depressive symptoms, over a range that spanned the usual cutoff point of 16 for diagnosing clinical depression, were more likely to have securely attached infants. Infants of mothers reporting the least depressive symptoms were more likely to show avoidant attachment, while infants of mothers with the most severe depressive symptoms were likely to show either avoidant or unstable avoidant attachment. Unstable avoidance refers to a pattern of behavior in which marked avoidance of the mother at the first reunion is replaced by proximity or contact-seeking at the second reunion. This pattern was found to be associated also with infant maltreatment (Lyons-Ruth, Connell, Zoll, and Stahl, in press).

Consistent with the findings of Spieker and Booth (1985) and Radke-Yarrow and others (1985) regarding the association of the A/C pattern with maternal depression, mothers of unstable avoidant infants in our sample were more depressed than other mothers in the sample ($F(1,54) = 3.17$, $p < .08$). Only two infants showed the resistant/attachment pattern in this sample, and their mothers reported low to moderate depression scores of 5 and 18.

It is not surprising that infant avoidance, including unstable avoidance, was found to be more frequent among infants of depressed mothers, since previous analyses had indicated that depressed mothers exhibit more covert hostility and since covert hostility was found to be related to infant avoidance, including unstable avoidance (Lyons-Ruth, Connell, Zoll, and Stahl, in press).

The increase in infant avoidance among the least depressed mothers is more puzzling but does fit with our hypothesis that mothers giving zero scores on the depression scale might fit Main's description of the rigidly controlled mothers likely to have avoidant infants. All three mothers giving zero depression scores had avoidant infants. A number of other mothers reporting low depression scores also had avoidant infants, but they did not show marked signs of the negative interactive behaviors characterizing both the zero-score mothers and the highly depressed mothers. Thus, the curvilinear relationship between insecure attachment and depression is consistent with, but not completely explained by, the maternal behaviors when the infants observed were twelve months old.

Discussion

Among women of very low socioeconomic status, depression appears to be a frequent concomitant of motherhood. Close to a third of low-income mothers without obvious parenting problems reported serious depressive symptoms, while almost two-thirds of mothers having problems relating to their infants were depressed. Furthermore, these serious depressive symptoms did not change over the six to eighteen months between our two assessments, despite the documented sensitivity of depression scales to effects of therapeutic intervention or positive life change (Murphy, 1981). This is congruent with the report by Brown and Harris (1975) that lower-class women have a much higher rate of chronic depression (symptoms lasting more than a year) than do middle-class women. Thus, at least during the periods of their child's infancy, many mothers in the sample were chronically depressed.

Maternal depressive symptoms in our sample were more strongly related to aspects of the mothers' family and peer relationships growing up than to current demographic characteristics. Thus, the substantial variation in maternal depression that does exist within a very economically stressed sample is more highly related to important aspects of early relationships, such as parental warmth, placement in foster care, presence of parental psychopathology, or adequacy of peer relationships, than to such current demographic characteristics as income or educational level. Conversely, positive early peer and family experiences are related to an absence of maternal depression, even under serious economic stress. These data provide some support for the view that the effects of serious family dysfunction in one generation may be traced into the second and third generations via the effects of maternal depression reported here, lending additional importance to the study of family interactions involving depressed parents.

Brown and Harris (1975) have shown that the presence of a close confidant can protect against depression even among low-SES mothers of young children. Thus, the hypothesis regarding the effects of family history is that satisfying early relationships facilitate the formation of confiding relationships as adults. Therefore, these associations between early life experiences and current depression may be mediated through the quality of current relationships, a link that has not yet been assessed.

By the time infants were a year old, interactions between depressed mothers and their infants, as assessed in this study, had taken on the negative qualities previously reported in studies of mother-child interaction between latency-aged and adolescent children and their depressed mothers. For example, Weissman and Paykel (1974) reported that depressed women were more irritable and resentful of their children, as well as less affectionate and involved with them than were women in the same neighborhood who were not psychiatrically ill. Belle (1982) similarly reported that depressed low-income women were more critical and demanding and less warm and responsive than low-income women who were not depressed. Weissman and Paykel further reported that the mother's negative interaction patterns with their children persisted even after the acute depressive symptoms had been resolved, and Weissman and others (1984) found that children of depressed women incurred a threefold risk of psychiatric disorder in childhood compared to children of controls. Thus, these early negative patterns of interaction between depressed mothers and their infants are part of an interactive context with serious long-term consequences for child adjustment.

Short-term negative consequences were also evident, confirming the hypothesis that maternal depression is a risk factor for development during infancy. Infants of depressed mothers had lowered mental and motor development scores at one year of age, with differences between infants of the least depressed and most depressed mothers exceeding ten points on each scale. The relationship between maternal depression and lowered infant developmental scores occurred even with maternal IQ controlled, ruling out the possible interpretation that less intellectually capable mothers are both more depressed and have less capable infants. Maternal IQ was not associated with maternal depression in this sample, indicating that the association between maternal depression and lowered infant developmental scores occurred through another route.

Somewhat surprisingly, the effects of maternal depression on infant development could not be traced through our observational data on maternal behavior. The maternal behaviors most highly related to depression—namely, increased affectivity, hostility, and interference—did not relate either positively or negatively to infant mental or physical development at twelve months of age. Conversely, the maternal behaviors that did relate to infant development were those related to maternal IQ rather than to maternal depression. Perhaps the observational situation acted to mask those features of the behaviors of depressed women that impacted negatively on their infants' development, or perhaps maternal behaviors earlier in the first year were more important in influencing development than those assessed concurrently. For example, through the home visits conducted as a part of the intervention component of the study, we were aware that many mothers left their infants unattended in their cribs for long periods of time. This practice may be related both to the extent of the mother's depression and to slowed infant development, but it was not evident during the observational sessions at twelve months and so is not represented in our data.

Another intriguing possibility is suggested by the observations of a subset of these infants at six months of age presented in Chapter Three of this volume. Cohn, Matias, Tronick, Connell, and Lyons-Ruth found that a subset of mothers who were very uninvolved with their infants in the naturalistic observation became much more intrusive in the face-to-face interaction. Recent longitudinal analyses by Spencer, Lyons-Ruth, Cohn, Matias, and Connell (1986) have also revealed a subgroup of mothers in our sample who are very uninvolved during the six-month's home observation but who have become highly hostile and intrusive by the time their infants reach twelve months of age. Thus, there may be a subgroup of depressed mothers whose behavior is quite labile depending on the demand characteristics of the situation and the developmental stage of the infant; alternating disengagement with intrusive overstimulation may be common among these women. Whether such inconsistency is related to depressive symptomatology or is more characteristic of a particular subgroup of depressed mothers is a question for future researchers.

The severity of maternal depression also influenced the security of the infant's attachment to the mother by the time the infant was twelve months old. Mothers reporting mild to moderate depression were more likely to have securely attached infants, while mothers reporting severe depression were more likely to have infants showing unstable avoidant attachment. More surprisingly, mothers reporting the least frequent depressive symptoms were more likely to have avoidant infants.

The curvilinear relationship between depressive symptoms and security of attachment may again indicate the presence of particular subgroups within both the depressed and nondepressed groups that require further description. It is notable that mild to moderate levels of maternal depression were consistent with secure infant attachment. Radke-Yarrow and others (1985) have also reported that insecure infant attachment did not increase among mothers with minor depression, but a majority of infants of mothers with major depressive symptomatology were insecurely attached. This suggests that mothers with moderate levels of depression are still able to maintain an accepting stance toward their infants, relatively free of the hostile and intrusive behavior more characteristic of severely depressed mothers.

The heightened incidence of avoidant infant attachment behavior among two very different groups of mothers in the present sample—those reporting the most and least depressive symptoms—suggests that hostile and controlling maternal behavior may occur in the context of several different maternal personality configurations, with different socioeconomic, cultural, and psychiatric characteristics. Thus, infant avoidance of the mother at reunion has been reported to be more frequent among more rigid, rejecting, and covertly angry middle-class mothers (Ainsworth and others, 1978; Main and Weston, 1982), among highly interactive, "overstimulating" middle-class mothers (Belsky, Rovine, and Taylor, 1984), among North German middle-class mothers engaging in culturally prescribed "independence training" when infants are one year old (Grossman, Grossman, Spangler, Suess, and Unzner, 1985), and among maltreating mothers (Lamb, Gaensbauer, Malkin, and Schultz, 1985; Lyons-Ruth, Connell, Zoll, and Stahl, in press), as well as among highly depressed mothers. Since the repertoire of infant behavior is relatively limited compared to maternal behavior, it is perhaps not surprising that relatively few infant behavioral responses are associated with a wider variety of maternal personality and behavioral patterns, patterns that have dissimilar as well as similar features.

While the maternal interactive behaviors associated with infant avoidance have shown some consistency over studies (as noted above), we need to study further the maternal interactive behaviors that differentiate the stable avoidant behavior noted in low-risk middle-class samples from the more disorganized forms of unstable avoidant and avoidant/resistant behavior noted among infants of maltreating and severely depressed mothers. Both stable and unstable avoidance were associated with hostile and intrusive maternal behavior in our sample.

A major conceptual issue latent in the discussion of these results is whether and when quantitative linear models are useful to apply to depression data. Hinde and Dennis (1985) have discussed similar issues regarding the use of the linear model in relation to studies of early social development. For example, in our study, maternal depression is a symptom that occurs in a variety of very differently organized personality or diagnostic configurations within descriptive psychiatry, including bipolar affective disorder, major depression, dysthymic disorder, alcohol and drug abuse, and borderline personality disorder. Thus, whether maternal depression occurring within these very different personality or symptom organizations can be arranged along a linear continuum to predict infant behavior and development is a question about the usefulness of the linear conception, as well as a question about the impact of maternal depression. To some extent this is an empirical question: To what extent do linear treatments bring order to the data?

In our study, the linear treatment of maternal depression data was very useful in accounting for infant developmental achievements over their first year of life and in accounting for aspects of maternal interactive behavior and infant attachment. These data indicate that the concept of depression may organize data usefully across conventional diagnostic categories.

When linear treatments bring very little order to the data, however, there are a variety of other models that must be considered and tested, such as ordinal models, curvilinear models, or the presence in the data set of several discrete groups, each with a characteristic organizational pattern for the variables under study, with no one variable arranging the groups in a particular ordering. It is this last possibility that appears most likely to apply to the relationship between maternal characteristics and infant attachment and that provides the greatest conceptual and analytical challenge to the investigator of the high-risk mothers and children.

References

Ainsworth, M.D.S., Blehar, M., Waters, E., and Wall, S. *Patterns of Attachment.* Hillsdale, N.J.: Erlbaum, 1978.

Bayley, N. *The Bayley Scales of Infant Development.* New York: The Psychological Corporation, 1969.

Belle, D. *Lives in Stress: Women and Depression.* Beverly Hills, Calif.: Sage, 1982.

Belsky, J., Rovine, M., and Taylor, D. "The Pennsylvania Infant and Family Development Project, III: The Origins of Individual Differences in Infant-Mother Attachment—Maternal and Infant Contributions." *Child Development,* 1984, *55,* 718-728.

Boyd, J. H., and Weissman, M. M. "Epidemiology of Affective Disorders: A Reexamination and Future Directions." *Archives of General Pscyhiatry,* 1981, *38,* 1039-1046.

Broman, A., Nichols, R., and Kennedy, W. *Preschool IQ: Prenatal and Early Developmental Correlates.* Hillsdale, N.J.: Erlbaum, 1975.

Brown, G., and Harris, T. *Social Origins of Depression: A Study of Psychiatric Disorders in Women.* New York: Free Press, 1975.

Comstock, G. W., and Helsing, K. J. "Symptoms of Depression in Two Communities." *Psychological Medicine,* 1976, *6,* 551-563.

Cronbach, L. "Coefficient Alpha and the Internal Structure of Tests." *Psychometrika,* 1951, *16,* 297-334.

Crook, T., Raskin, A., and Eliot, J. "Parent-Child Relationships and Adult Depression." *Child Development,* 1981, *52,* 950-957.

Dohrenwend, B. P., and Dohrenwend, B. S. *Social Status and Psychological Disorder: A Causal Inquiry.* New York: Wiley, 1969.

Fisher, L., Harder, D., and Kokes, R. "Child Competence and Psychiatric Risk: III. Comparisons Based on Diagnosis of Hospitalized Parent." *Journal of Nervous and Mental Disorders,* 1980, *168* (6), 338-342.

Grossmann, K., Grossmann, K. E., Spangler, G., Suess, G., and Unzner, L. "Maternal Sensitivity and Newborn's Orientation Responses as Related to Quality of Attachment in Northern Germany." In I. Bretheron and E. Waters (eds.), *Growing Points in Attachment Theory and Research. Monographs of the Society for Research in Child Development,* No. 209, 1985 *50* (1-2), 233-256.

Grunebaum, J., Cohler, B., Kauffman, C., and Gallant, D. "Children of Depressed and Schizophrenic Mothers." *Child Psychiatry and Human Development*, 1978, *8* (4), 219-229.

Hinde, R. A., and Dennis, A. "Categorizing Individuals: A Method Linking Clinical and Developmental Psychology." Paper presented at the biennial meeting of the Society for Research in Child Development, Toronto, April 1985.

Hollingshead, A. B. *Four-Factor Index of Social Status.* Unpublished manuscript. New Haven, Conn.: Yale University. 1975.

Husaini, B. A., Neff, T. A., Harrington, J. B., Hughes, M. D., and Stone, R. H. "Depression in Rural Communities: Validating the CES-D Scale." *Journal of Community Psychology*, 1980, *8*, 20-27.

Kokes, R., Harder, D., Fisher, L., and Strauss, J. "Child Competence and Psychiatric Risk: V. Sex of Patient Parent and Dimensions of Psychopathology." *The Journal of Nervous and Mental Disorders*, 1980, *168* (6), 348-352.

Lamb, M. E., Gaensbauer, T. J., Malkin, C. M., and Schultz, L. A. "The Effects of Child Maltreatment on Security of Infant-Adult Attachment." *Infant Behavior and Development*, 1985, *8*, 35-45.

Lyons-Ruth, K., Botein, S., and Grunebaum, H. "Reaching the Hard-to-Reach: Serving Multirisk Families with Infants in the Community." In B. J. Cohler and J. S. Musick (eds.), *Intervention with Psychiatrically Disabled Parents and Their Young Children.* New Directions for Mental Health Services, no. 24. San Francisco: Jossey-Bass, 1984.

Lyons-Ruth, K., Connell, D., Grunebaum, H., Botein, S., and Zoll, D. "Maternal Family History, Maternal Caretaking, and Infant Attachment in Multiproblem Families." *Preventive Psychiatry*, 1984, *2* (3-4), 403-425.

Lyons-Ruth, K., Connell, D., Zoll, D., and Stahl, J. "Infants at Social Risk: Relations Among Infant Maltreatment, Maternal Behavior, and Infant Attachment Behavior." *Developmental Psychology*, in press.

Main, M., and Weston, D. R. "Avoidance of the Attachment Figure in Infancy: Descriptions and Interpretations." In C. M. Parkes and J. Stevenson-Hinde (eds.), *The Place of Attachment in Human Behavior.* New York: Basic Books, 1982.

Murphy, J. *Psychiatric Instrument Development for Primary Care Research: Patient Self-Report Questionnaire.* Final Report, NIMH Contract No. 80M0142-80101D. Rockville, Md.: Division of Biometry and Epidemiology, National Institute of Mental Health, 1981.

Myers, J. K., and Weissman, M. M. "Use of Self-Report Symptom Scale to Detect Depression in a Community Sample." *American Journal of Psychiatry*, 1980, *137* (9), 1081-1083.

Radke-Yarrow, M., Cummings, E. M., Kuczynski, L., and Chapman, M. "Patterns of Attachment in Two- and Three-Year-Olds in Normal Families and Families with Parental Depression." *Child Development*, 1985, *56*, 884-893.

Radloff, L. S. "The CES-D Scale: A Self-Report Depression Scale for Research in the General Population." *Applied Psychological Measurement*, 1977, *1*, 385-401.

Rolf, J. E., Crowther, J., Teri, L., and Bond, L. "Contrasting Developmental Risks in Preschool Children of Psychiatrically Hospitalized Parents." In N. F. Watt, E. J. Anthony, L. C. Wynne, and J. E. Rolf (eds.), *Children at Risk for Schizophrenia: A Longitudinal Perspective.* Cambridge, England: Cambridge University Press, 1984.

Rutter, M. "Protective Factors in Children's Responses to Stress and Disadvantage." In M. W. Kent and T. W. Rolf (eds.), *Social Competence in Children.* Hanover, N.H.: University Press of New England, 1979.

Rutter, M., Yule, B., Quinton, D., Rowlands, O., Yule, W., and Berger, M. "Attainment and Adjustment in Two Geographical Areas, III: Some Factors Accounting for Area Differences." *British Journal of Psychiatry*, 1975, *126*, 520-533.

Sameroff, A. J., and Chandler, M. J. "Reproductive Risk and the Continuum of Caretaking Casualty." In F. D. Horowitz, M. Hetherington, S. Scarr-Salapatek, and G. Seigel (eds.), *Review of Child Development Research*. Vol. 4. Chicago: University of Chicago Press, 1975.

Sameroff, A. J., Seifer, R., and Zax, M. "Early Development of Children at Risk for Emotional Disorder." *Monographs of the Society for Research in Child Development*, No. 199, 1982, *47* (7), entire issue.

Spencer, T., Lyons-Ruth, K., Cohn, T., Matias, R., and Connell, D. "Infants at Social Risk: Mother-Infant Interaction at Seven Months of Age and Its Relation to Later Infant Attachment Behavior." Unpublished paper. Cambridge, Mass.: Harvard Medical School, 1986.

Spieker, S. J., and Booth, C. L. "Family Risk Typologies and Patterns of Insecure Attachment." In J. D. Osofsky (Chair), *Intervention with Infants at Risk: Patterns of Attachment*. Symposium presented at the biennial meeting of the Society for Research in Child Development, Toronto, April 1985.

Wechsler, D. *Wechsler Adult Intelligence Scale Manual*. New York: The Psychological Corporation, 1955.

Weissman, M. M., Myers, J. K., and Thompson, W. D. "Depression and Its Treatment in a U.S. Urban Community: 1975-1976." *Archives of General Psychiatry*, 1981, *38*, 417-421.

Weissman, M. M., and Paykel, E. S. *The Depressed Woman: A Study of Social Relationships*. Chicago: University of Chicago Press, 1974.

Weissman, M. M., Prusoff, B. A., Gammon, G. D., Merikangas, K., Leckman, J., and Kidd, K. "Psychopathology in the Children (Ages Six-Eighteen) of Depressed and Normal Parents." *Journal of the American Academy of Child Psychiatry*, 1984, *23* (1), 78-84.

Weissman, M. M., Sholomskas, D., Pottenger, M., Prusoff, B. A., and Locke, B. Z. "Assessing Depressive Symptoms in Five Psychiatric Populations: A Validation Study." *American Journal of Epidemiology*, 1977, *106*, 203-214.

Karlen Lyons-Ruth is instructor in psychology in the Department of Psychiatry, Harvard Medical School, Cambridge Hospital. Her research interests have focused on the social and emotional development of normal and high-risk infants.

David Zoll is a psychology fellow in the Department of Psychiatry, Harvard Medical School, Cambridge Hospital, and a doctoral candidate in the Psychology Department at Boston University.

David Connell is a lecturer in psychology in the Department of Psychiatry, Harvard Medical School, Cambridge Hospital, and a series analyst at Abt Associates, Cambridge, Massachusetts.

Henry U. Grunebaum is professor of psychiatry, Harvard Medical School, Cambridge Hospital.

Index

A

Achenbach, T. M., 18, 22, 26, 27
Adamson, L., 27, 53, 60
Aid to Families of Dependent Children (AFDC), 68
Ainsworth, M.D.S., 22, 27, 50, 58, 65, 66, 74, 79, 80
Ainsworth Strange Situation, 21-22, 65-66, 75
Als, H., 13, 18, 27, 35, 44, 53, 60
Arend, R. A., 32, 43
Avoidant/resistant (A/C) infants, 75

B

Bakeman, R., 38, 42, 53, 58
Baldwin, A. L., 32, 42
Baldwin, C. P., 42
Barnett, C., 29
Bartko, J. J., 52, 58
Bates, J. E., 18, 22, 23, 27, 32, 42
Bayley, N., 65, 80
Bayley Scales of Infant Development, 65, 71, 75
Beardslee, W. R., 13, 21, 27, 32, 42
Beck, A. T., 53, 58
Beck depression inventory, 56
Beckwith, L., 18, 22, 27
Belle, D., 15, 27, 70, 77, 80
Belsky, J., 79, 80
Bemporad, J., 27, 42
Berger, M., 44, 82
Bhrolchain, M. N., 28
Blehar, M., 27, 65, 66, 80
Bond, L., 62, 81
Booth, C. L., 75, 82
Born, W. S., 56, 59
Botein, S., 64, 81
Bowlby, J., 21, 27
Bowlby, T. B., 48, 50, 58
Boyd, J. H., 61, 80
Brazelton, B., 27, 35, 44, 53, 56, 58, 60
Brazelton Neonatal Assessment, 56
Breese, G. R., 50, 58
Broman, A., 63, 80
Bromet, E., 13, 16, 17, 27
Brown, G. W., 13, 18, 20, 24, 28, 61, 68, 76, 77, 80
Brown, J. V., 38, 42, 53, 58
Bruner, J. S., 33, 42, 43

C

Campos, J. J., 33, 42
Center for Epidemiological Studies Depression Scale (CES-D), 34, 64, 66, 67, 68, 71, 73
Chandler, M. J., 63, 82
Chapman, M., 43, 81
Chess, S., 18, 22, 29, 30
Chi-square test, 64, 68
Child Behavior Profile, 22
Clarke-Stewart, K. A., 32, 42, 51, 58
Coe, C. L., 48, 59
Cohen, S. E., 18, 27
Cohler, B. J., 31, 42, 43, 61, 81
Cohn, J. F., 13, 28, 32, 33, 39, 41, 42, 44, 53, 55, 56, 58, 60
Cohn, T., 78, 82
Cole, R. E., 42
Collins, J. L., 60
Comstock, G. W., 64, 66, 80
Connell, D., 36, 42, 43, 64, 65, 66, 75, 76, 79, 81, 82
Cornely, M.P.H., 13, 16, 17, 27
Crichton, L., 32, 44
Cronbach, L., 65, 80
Cronbach's *Alpha*, 65
Crook, T., 70, 80
Crowther, J., 61, 81
Cullen, J. S., 52, 59
Cummings, E. M., 43, 44, 81
Cytryn, L., 32, 43, 52, 58

D

Davidson, J. R., 56, 58
Dempsey, J., 53, 59
Dennis, A., 79, 81
Depression: and family history, 70; in general population, 15; of women, 62. *See also* Maternal depression

83

Diagnostic and Statistical Manual of the American Psychiatric Association, DSM-III, 15, 16
Dohrenwend, B. P., 63, 80
Dohrenwend, B. S., 63, 80
Dunn, L., 28

E

Earls, F. J., 16, 17–18, 23, 24, 28
Eaton, W. W., 15, 28
Edelbrock, C. S., 22, 26, 27
Egeland, B., 32, 44
Eliot, J., 70, 80
Elliot, S. A., 15, 28
Emde, R. N., 50, 58
Emotions: and infant activity, 6; mothers' influence on infant, 7–9; and regulatory displays, 6–7; and self-stimulating behaviors, 6
Endicott, J., 29, 34, 44
Engel, G. L., 50, 58
Epidemiologic Catchment Area (ECA), 16
Erbaugh, J., 53, 58

F

F-test, 64
Fafouti-Milenković, M., 36, 43
Family Support Project, 34
Feighner, J. P., 16, 28
Feighner criteria, 16
Feiring, C., 21, 29
Field, R., 13, 18, 28
Field, T., 33, 36, 38, 43, 48, 51, 52, 53, 56, 58, 59
Fisher, L., 61, 80, 81
Fogel, A., 36, 37, 43
Frankel, K. A., 22, 27, 42

G

Gaensbauer, T. J., 31, 43, 79, 81
Gallant, D. H., 42, 43, 61, 81
Gamer, E., 31, 42, 43
Gammon, G. D., 30, 82
Garcia, R., 56, 59
Garrison, W. T., 16, 17–18, 23, 28
Gershon, E. S., 32, 43
Ghodsian, M., 16, 20–21, 26, 28, 30
Gianino, A. F., Jr., 5, 11
Goldberg, S., 18, 29

Goldstein, S., 56, 59
Gottman, J. M., 39, 43
Graham, P., 19, 29
Grossman, K. E., 79, 80
Grundy, P. F., 56, 59
Grunebaum, H. U., 42, 43, 64, 82
Grunebaum, J., 61, 81
Guy, L., 56, 59
Guze, S. B., 28

H

Hailey, A., 29
Hamovitt, J., 52, 58
Harder, D., 61, 80
Harder, S., 61, 80
Harlow, H. F., 48, 59, 60
Harmon, R. J., 43, 50, 58
Harrington, J. B., 81
Harris, R., 61, 68, 76, 77, 80
Harris, T., 18, 20, 28
Harter, S., 24, 29
Hay, R. A., 39, 43
Helsing, K. J., 64, 66, 80
Hinde, R. A., 79, 81
Hollingshead, A. B., 65, 81
Howard, J. L., 50, 55, 58, 59
Hughes, M. D., 81
Husaini, B. A., 64, 66, 81

I

Infants: active coping of, 50–51; attachment and pathology of, 21–23, 75–76; behavior and maternal depression, 20–21, 52–57; bonding of, 22–23; developmental problems of, 40, 71; early separation experiences of, 48–50; face-to-face behavior of, 33–34; fathers' affect on, 51, 62; interaction with mother, 7–9; other-directed behavior of, 7; passive coping of, 55; prior depression of, 56; psychopathology of, 10; reactive depression in, 51–52; reunion interactions of, 54–55; self-regulation of, 6–7; and siblings, 49–50; social interaction of, 33; and stress, 50; temperament disorders of, 18–19
International Classification and Diagnostic System of the World Health Organization (ICD-9), 16

J

James, S., 15, 29
Jaskir, J., 21, 29

K

Kaplan, D. N., 18, 29
Kauffman, C., 61, 81
Kaufman, I. C., 48, 59
Kaye, K., 36, 37, 43
Keller, M. B., 27, 42
Kendall, R. E., 18, 29
Kennedy, W., 63, 80
Kessler, I. G., 15, 28
Kidd, K., 30, 82
Kindlon, D., 23, 28
Klein, R. P., 44
Klerman, G. L., 27, 42
Koenig, K. L., 50, 58
Kokes, R., 61, 80
Kuczynski, L., 43, 81

L

Lamb, M. E., 51, 59, 79, 81
Lamour, M., 43, 52, 58
Lawler, J. E., 55, 59
Leckman, J., 30, 82
Legg, C., 51, 59
Leiderman, P., 29
Leifer, A., 18, 29
Leonard, M. A., 30
Levine, S., 48, 59
Lewis, I., 13, 16, 18, 29
Lewis, J. K., 50, 58
Lewis, M., 13, 21, 22, 29
Links, P. S., 17, 29
Lipton, M. A., 50, 58
Locke, B. Z., 82
Lunde, D., 30
Lyons-Ruth, K., 36, 42, 43, 64, 65, 66, 75, 76, 78, 79, 81, 82

M

McCabe, P., 50, 51, 55, 59
McCarthy, M. E., 44
McCleary, R., 39, 43
McCrary, M. D., 30
McGuffog, C., 21, 29
McKinney, W. T., 50, 58
McKnew, D. H., 43, 44, 52, 58
McQuiston, S., 44
MacTurk, R. H., 44
Main, M., 79, 81
Malkin, C. M., 79, 81
Manning, J., 55, 59
Martha's Vineyard Child Health Survey, 23-25
Martin, E. B., 56, 59
Martin, P. L., 55, 56, 59
Maslin, C. A., 22, 27, 42
Mason, E. A., 18, 29
Matas, L., 32, 43
Maternal depression: assessment of, 64; care providers' effect on, 66-67; child's temperament and, 18-19; correlates of, 17-19; cultural factors and, 15-16, 18, 63; denial of, 71; disordered children and, 18, 20; Family Support Project Study of, 34-41; genetic factors in, 55-56; and hospitalization, 67-68; infant attachment and, 75-76; infant behavior and, 52-57; infant development and, 71-75; and IQ, 72, 77; marital conflict and, 17; Martha's Vineyard study of, 23-27; maternal affect and, 36-41; maternal family history of, 65, 70; maternal hostility and, 40-41; positive results of, 10; postpartum, 15, 56; prevalence rates of, 15-17; screening techniques for, 42; simulated, 33-34, 53; socioeconomic factors and, 15-16, 63, 66-67; and stress, 17-18, 63; study of, and low socioeconomic status, 64-80; in United Kingdom, 19-21; and welfare, 68; young children as cause of, 16-17
Matias, R., 42, 78, 82
Mendelson, M., 53, 58
Merikangas, K. R., 30, 82
Metcalf, D., 50, 58
Mock, J. E., 53, 58
Moos, R., 30
Moss, P., 13, 16, 18, 29
Mother: angry behavior of, 35-36; communication of affect of, 9, 32, 36-41, 56; fit of, with child, 18; and infant bonding, 22-23; intrusive behavior of, 35-36, 40-41; role of, in regulation, 7; schizophrenic, 62, 67

Mother-infant interaction: with depressed mothers, 9-10; with difficult child, 18; impact of, 8-9; and infant regulation, 8-10; and mutual responsiveness, 39; positive effects of, 8; structured, 39. *See also* Infants; Mother

Mother-infant separation: biphasic response in, 48-50; and heart rate, 50-51, 55; human studies of, 48-55; physiological effects of, 50; primate studies of, 48, 55; primate versus human, 52

Mueller, R. A., 50, 58
Muñoz, R., 28
Murphy, D. L., 56, 59
Murphy, J., 76, 81

Mutual Regulation Model (MRM): depression and, 9-10; mothers' role in, 7; other-directed regulation in, 7; self-regulation in, 5-6

Myers, J. K., 34, 43, 61, 64, 67, 68, 81, 82

N

Neff, T. A., 81
Nichols, A., 63, 80
Nicklas, N., 28
Nurnberger, J., 32, 43

O

Obrist, P. A., 50, 55, 59
Occupational Scale from the Hollingshead Four-Factor Index of Social Status, 65
Orr, S. T., 15, 29
Other-directed regulation, by infant, 7

P

Parke, R., 51, 59
Pauley, J. D., 48, 55, 59
Paykel, E. S., 32, 35, 36, 44, 70, 77, 82
Perceived Competence Scale for Young Children, 24
Plomin, R., 19, 29
Postpartum depression, 15, 56. *See also* Maternal depression
Pottenger, M., 82

Prange, A. J., 50, 58
Primate infant studies, 48-49, 52
Prusoff, B. A., 30, 82

Q

Quinton, D., 44, 82

R

Radke-Yarrow, M., 31, 32, 43, 44, 75, 78, 81
Radloff, L. S., 34, 43, 64, 81
Rapid eye movement (REM) sleep, 48
Raskin, A., 70, 80
Ratner, N. K., 33, 43
Reite, M., 48, 50, 51, 52, 55, 59
Research Diagnostic Criteria, 16, 34, 42
Richman, N., 13, 16, 18, 19, 20, 29
Ricks, M., 56, 60
Roberts, C. J., 56, 59
Robertson, J., 48, 59
Robins, E., 28, 29, 33, 44
Robins, L., 34, 44
Rochester study, 61
Rolf, J. E., 61, 81
Rovine, M., 79, 80
Rowlands, O., 44, 82
Rugg, A. J., 28
Rutter, M., 34, 44, 61, 63, 81, 82

S

Sameroff, A., 31, 32, 41, 44
Sameroff, A. J., 63, 82
Sameroff, A. V., 52, 55, 59
Sandberg, D., 56, 59
Sander, L., 33, 44
Schaeffer, S., 13, 29
Schmale, A. H., 50, 58
Schneiderman, N., 50, 51, 55, 59
Schultz, L. A., 79, 81
Seashore, M., 18, 29
Seifer, R., 44, 52, 55, 59, 63, 82
Seiler, C., 52, 55, 59
Self-regulation: and child psychopathology, 11; and infant self-stimulating behavior, 6; by older infants, 10; by six-month-old infants, 9
Self-stimulating behavior. *See* Self-regulation

Separation. *See* Mother-infant separation
Shannon, B., 29
Shea, E., 33, 44
Sherick, I., 51, 59
Sholomaskas, D., 82
Short, R., 48, 55, 59
Shuman, H. H., 53, 59
Siblings. *See* Infants
Sleep disturbances, 48
Smith, R. D., 50, 58
Smith, R. S., 13, 30
Smithson, K. W., 55, 59
Snyder, D. S., 48, 52, 59
Socioeconomic status (SES), 34, 62, 63, 68
Solomon, Z., 28
Sostek, A. J., 56, 59
Sostek, A. M., 56, 59
Spangler, G., 79, 80
Spencer, T., 78, 82
Spieker, S. J., 75, 82
Spitz, R., 59
Spitzer, R. L., 16, 29, 34, 44
Sroufe, L. A., 32, 43
Stahl, J., 36, 43, 64, 65, 66, 75, 76, 79, 81
Staff, M. D., 22, 29
Stenberg, C., 33, 42
Stevenson, J., 19, 29
Stone, R. H., 81
Strauss, J., 61, 81
Stress: infants and, 50–51, 55; and maternal depression, 17–18, 63
Stynes, A. J., 48, 59
Suess, G., 79, 80
Suomi, S. J., 48, 60

T

Taraldson, B., 32, 44
Taylor, D., 79, 80
Teri, L., 62, 81
Thomas, A., 18, 22, 29, 30
Thompson, W. D., 61, 82
Tronick, E. Z., 5, 11, 13, 27, 32–33, 35, 39, 43, 44, 53, 55, 56, 58, 60

U

Unzer, L., 79, 80
Uzgiris, I. Č., 36, 43

V

Vaughn, B. E., 32, 44
Vega-Lahr, N., 56, 59
Vietze, P. M., 44

W

Wadland, W., 51, 59
Wagonfield, S., 50, 58
Wainwright, S., 29
Wall, S., 27, 65, 66, 80
Waltham Forest Family Register, 19
Ward, C. H., 53, 58
Waters, E., 27, 65, 66, 80
Watson, J. P., 28
Wechsler, D., 65, 82
Wechsler Adult Intelligence Scale (WAIS), 65
Weintraub, M., 18, 30
Weiss, J. L., 42
Weissman, M. M., 13, 30, 32, 34, 35, 36, 43, 44, 61, 64, 66, 68, 70, 77, 80, 81, 82
Welner, A., 13, 30
Werner, E., 13, 30
Weston, D. R., 81
Williams, J., 29
Winokur, G., 28
Wise, S., 53, 60
Wolf, B. M., 18, 30
Wolkind, S., 20, 28, 30
Woodruff, R. A., 28

Y

Yalom, I., 15, 30
Yarrow, L. J., 41, 44
Yogman, M. W., 51, 60
Young, L. D., 50, 58
Yule, W., 44, 82

Z

Zahn-Waxler, C., 31, 43, 44
Zajicek, E., 28, 30
Zajicek-Coleman, E., 29
Zax, M., 44, 63, 82
Zimmerman, J., 52, 59
Zoll, D., 36, 43, 64, 65, 66, 75, 76, 79, 81

U.S. Postal Service
STATEMENT OF OWNERSHIP, MANAGEMENT AND CIRCULATION
Required by 39 U.S.C. 3685

1A. TITLE OF PUBLICATION	1B. PUBLICATION NO.	2. DATE OF FILING
New Directions for Child Development	4 9 4 0 9 0 0	9/26/86

3. FREQUENCY OF ISSUE	3A. NO. OF ISSUES PUBLISHED ANNUALLY	3B. ANNUAL SUBSCRIPTION PRICE
Quarterly	4	$30 indv/$40 inst

4. COMPLETE MAILING ADDRESS OF KNOWN OFFICE OF PUBLICATION *(Street, City, County, State and ZIP+4 Code) (Not printers)*
433 California St., San Francisco (SF County), CA 94104

5. COMPLETE MAILING ADDRESS OF THE HEADQUARTERS OF GENERAL BUSINESS OFFICES OF THE PUBLISHER *(Not printer)*
433 California St., San Francisco (SF County), CA 94104

6. FULL NAMES AND COMPLETE MAILING ADDRESS OF PUBLISHER, EDITOR, AND MANAGING EDITOR *(This item MUST NOT be blank)*

PUBLISHER *(Name and Complete Mailing Address)*
Jossey-Bass Inc., Publishers, 433 California St., San Francisco, CA 94104

EDITOR *(Name and Complete Mailing Address)*
William Damon, Dept. of Psychology, Clark University, Worcester, MA 01610

MANAGING EDITOR *(Name and Complete Mailing Address)*
William Henry, Jossey-Bass Publishers, 433 California St., S.F., CA 94104

7. OWNER *(If owned by a corporation, its name and address must be stated and also immediately thereunder the names and addresses of stockholders owning or holding 1 percent or more of total amount of stock. If not owned by a corporation, the names and addresses of the individual owners must be given. If owned by a partnership or other unincorporated firm, its name and address, as well as that of each individual must be given. If the publication is published by a nonprofit organization, its name and address must be stated.) (Item must be completed.)*

FULL NAME	COMPLETE MAILING ADDRESS
Jossey-Bass Inc., Publishers	433 California St., S.F., CA 94104

8. KNOWN BONDHOLDERS, MORTGAGEES, AND OTHER SECURITY HOLDERS OWNING OR HOLDING 1 PERCENT OR MORE OF TOTAL AMOUNT OF BONDS, MORTGAGES OR OTHER SECURITIES *(If there are none, so state)*

For names and addresses of stockholders, see attached list

FULL NAME	COMPLETE MAILING ADDRESS
Same as #7	

9. FOR COMPLETION BY NONPROFIT ORGANIZATIONS AUTHORIZED TO MAIL AT SPECIAL RATES *(Section 423.12 DMM only)*
The purpose, function, and nonprofit status of this organization and the exempt status for Federal income tax purposes (Check one)

☐ (1) HAS NOT CHANGED DURING PRECEDING 12 MONTHS
☐ (2) HAS CHANGED DURING PRECEDING 12 MONTHS
(If changed, publisher must submit explanation of change with this statement.)

10. EXTENT AND NATURE OF CIRCULATION	AVERAGE NO. COPIES EACH ISSUE DURING PRECEDING 12 MONTHS	ACTUAL NO. COPIES OF SINGLE ISSUE PUBLISHED NEAREST TO FILING DATE
A. TOTAL NO. COPIES *(Net Press Run)*	1300	1326
B. PAID AND/OR REQUESTED CIRCULATION		
1. Sales through dealers and carriers, street vendors and counter sales	148	37
2. Mail Subscription *(Paid and/or requested)*	484	534
C. TOTAL PAID AND/OR REQUESTED CIRCULATION *(Sum of 10B1 and 10B2)*	632	571
D. FREE DISTRIBUTION BY MAIL, CARRIER OR OTHER MEANS SAMPLES, COMPLIMENTARY, AND OTHER FREE COPIES	60	190
E. TOTAL DISTRIBUTION *(Sum of C and D)*	692	761
F. COPIES NOT DISTRIBUTED 1. Office use, left over, unaccounted, spoiled after printing	608	565
2. Return from News Agents		
G. TOTAL *(Sum of E, F1 and 2—should equal net press run shown in A)*	1300	1326

11. I certify that the statements made by me above are correct and complete

SIGNATURE AND TITLE OF EDITOR, PUBLISHER, BUSINESS MANAGER, OR OWNER
[signature] Vice President

PS Form 3526, Dec. 1985 *(See instruction on reverse)*

From the Editors' Notes

Evidence has accumulated that maternal depression is related to affective and cognitive disturbance in infants. This volume of New Directions for Child Development *presents reviews and recent research on the effects of maternal depression on infants and young children. It includes reviews of the epidemiology of maternal depression, studies on the distortions of interactions between depressed mothers and their infants, models for reactive and chronic depression in infancy, and research demonstrating the effects of maternal depression on infant attachment behavior and cognitive competence. The laboratory research described in this volume promises to provide a basis for methods that will have clinical utility in the near future.*

JOSSEY-BASS

DATE DUE

Date Due